Psychological Research

an introduction

third edition

Consulting Editor:
L. Joseph Stone
Vassar College

Psychological Research

an introduction

ARTHUR J. BACHRACH

Naval Medical Research Institute

Random House New York

THIRD EDITION 9876543

Copyright © 1962, 1965, 1972 by Random House, Inc.

All rights reserved under International and Pan-American Copyright Conventions. Published in the United States by Random House, Inc., and simultaneously in Canada by Random House of Canada Limited, Toronto.

Library of Congress Cataloging in Publication Data

Bachrach, Arthur J
Psychological research.

Bibliography: p.
1. Psychological research.
BF76.5.B3 1972   150'.72   79-39767
ISBN 0-394-31706-8

Manufactured in the United States of America

It is customary to wait until the middle of a bullfight to dedicate the bull to someone in the audience. In this way it is known whether the bull is brave enough to be dedicated or not. Unfortunately, this is not possible with a book, and so I am taking this book by the horns and dedicating it to three prized friends and colleagues who have taught me about research: *Murray Sidman, Joel Greenspoon, and Frank Banghart.*

Preface to the Third Edition

The great American novelist James Branch Cabell once said that when his first book was published he kept going back to look at it to make certain the ink hadn't faded. My own similar fears have been assuaged by two editions, and now a third, which you hold before you. In addition there have been two therapeutic translations—one published in Madrid in Spanish, the other a Portuguese edition published in São Paolo. To be sure, the translators had some trouble, particularly with my Second Law, stated in the Preface to the First Edition: "Things take more time than they do."* In any case, I am deeply grateful for the reception the book has received and particularly for the opportunity to hear from students who have written to say they liked it or to argue a point with me, for it was, after all, written for them.

There have been many people over the years who have contributed importantly to this little book. Mrs. Marilyn Waide, then at the University of Virginia, applied her intelligence and diligence to the development of the first edition. Dr. Andrée Fleming-Holland, at the time of the second edition a valued research assistant, provided important help in the first revision, a manuscript that Mrs. Jane Little did much to improve by her typing and editorial work. For help in the present edition I am

---

* My First Law, also stated in the Preface to the First Edition, summed up the entire purpose of writing the book: *People don't usually do research the way people who write books about research say that people do research.*

indebted to Mrs. Peg Matzen, whose cogent comments and sincere interest are warmly acknowledged. I am also grateful to my good friend Dr. Bob Hoke for conversations that have been both interesting and provocative.

The dedication to my friends Murray Sidman, Joel Greenspoon, and Frank Banghart stands sincerely, with an important addendum:

This one is for my wife, Susan.

Contents

read only

1. Introduction   **15**
Curiosity, Accident, and Discovery   15
The Careful Casual   19
A Case of Serendipity   25
Preconceived Ideas: Hypothesis Myopia   32

2. Characteristics and Goals of Science   **36**
Some Important Characteristics of Science   36
The Goals of Science   38
Observation and Experiment   39
Reason from Experiment: Toward Order and Law   46
Prediction from Observation and Experiment   49
Measurement in Science   52

**3. Two Fundamental Methods of Research: The
Formal Theoretical and the Informal Theoretical**   **59**
Data, Hypothesis, Theory, and Law: The Formal
   Theoretical Method   59
Data, Hypothesitos, Order, and Law: The Informal
   Theoretical Method   68

4. The Problem of Definition   **74**
Three Levels of Definition   77
The Problem of Clarity   78
An Attempt at Clarity and Certainty: The
   Operational Definition   81
Inferred and Invented Concepts   87

5. **The Laboratory and the "Real World":**
   Animal and Human Research 89
   But Why Animals? 91
   The Analogue Error 95

6. **Ethical Considerations in Research** 100
   Ethics and Morality in Science 100
   Public Concern with Research 105
   Ethical Considerations in Animal Research 108
   Ethical Considerations in Human Research 109

7. **The Scientist and the Social Order** 122
   The Scientist's Communication to the Public 123
   The Scientist's Communication to Other Scientists 127
   Science and the Social Order 133

Bibliography 137

Suggested Further Reading 143

Index 145

Our science of man . . . is no longer an abstract thing that may be built up *a priori* and from general views; it is the universal experimental method applied to human life, and consequently the study of all the products within the sphere of its activity, above all of its spontaneous activity.

ERNEST RENAN
The Future of Science (1848)

Psychological Research

an introduction

Chapter One
Introduction

Research is *not* statistics. I am beginning this introduction to the study of psychological research with a negative statement because I feel that many students are scared away from the enjoyable pursuit of research because they equate it with tedium and involved statistical manipulations. This is not difficult to understand, for a student who picks up a book on research is likely to find that it is no more than a book on statistics in research design. This is not to disparage statistics in any way, but merely to indicate that statistics is a *tool* of research, a useful one to be sure, but no more than a technique for handling some (and not all) research data. I am going to deal with research from a different standpoint, briefly mentioning some of the basic features of research (such as control and experimental groups), but not making any attempt to introduce the student to statistical techniques. Rather, I want to concern myself with the origins of research, scientific method and practice, the meaning of data and theory, the ethical aspects of research with animal and human subjects, and, most important, with the curiosity of the scientist, his main attribute and his main source of pleasure. As the brilliant chemist Linus Pauling once observed, "Satisfaction of one's curiosity is one of the greatest sources of happiness in life."

Curiosity, Accident, and Discovery

Let's start with the curiosity of the scientist. Much research begins with accidental discovery. A scientist is working diligently in his laboratory with a particular problem and a particular goal in view when something happens, perhaps something goes wrong. Sir Alexander Fleming had this happen when he was trying to culture some bacteria. You will recall that a little green mold was present in a dish in which he was culturing bacteria, and that the bacteria had been killed. This had probably happened to many scientists before him who might have sworn under their breaths about the ruined experiment, tossed the culture into the refuse and started again to culture the bacteria.

But this would have been contrary to scientific method in its ideal. As we will see later, after a problem has been selected, the scientific method consists fundamentally of two parts: (1) the collection of data and (2) the establishment of a functional relationship among these data. For Fleming, and those before him, there were two basic data: a bacteria culture was destroyed and a green mold was present in the dish. This is the fact: A and B coexisted. Now, was there a functional relationship between these two? Did A (the mold) have any effect on B (the bacteria)? This is the beginning of the research, to manipulate the conditions under which A and B coexisted so that an answer might be obtained. If they were functionally related (that is, A had an effect on B) that would be one answer. If they were not and the coexistence was pure chance, that would also be an answer.

So Fleming started with an *observation*. To start his experiment he probably formulated some sort of *hypothesis* which might be stated roughly as follows: "The appearance of the green mold and the destruction of the colony of bacteria are related; the green mold was responsible for the destruction of the bacteria." From this point, he proceeded to an experiment to test his hypothesis. He might take the green mold and put a new colony of live bacteria in contact with it. The results of this experiment would either confirm or refute the hypothesis. If the second colony of bacteria also perished when in contact with the green mold, then the experimenter might feel more comfortable in assuming a causal relationship. There are other factors which might be taken into consideration, such as temperature changes, the presence or absence of sunlight. But for the moment, assuming that these variables have been controlled, the experiment would be to manipulate the green mold and the bacteria under various controlled conditions.

Of course, Fleming's research showed that the green mold was responsible for the bacterial destruction and penicillin emerged from his findings. I want to emphasize the most important aspect of this. Fleming discovered this green mold by *accident*; he was attempting to culture a particular colony of bacteria. A lesser man might have been irritated and annoyed at the death of the bacteria, would have ignored the mold, and washed the entire dish down the sink. The fact that Fleming did not do this illustrates one of the characteristics of a good scientist. He has his eyes open; he is never so bound up in a fixed path of experimentation that he is blinded to unusual events which may occur. B. F. Skinner (85)* in one of his "unformalized principles of science" says, "When you run onto something interesting, drop everything else and study it." While this may not fit the image of science and the scientist that the student has conceived, it does illustrate the way much research originates and develops. To the person looking at science, it is often perceived as a logical, consistent, highly organized body of information revolving around a hard core of rigid prespecified methodology. J. Z. Young in his treatise on science (101) had the following to say:

One of the characteristics of scientists and their work, curiously enough, is a confusion, almost a muddle. This may seem strange if you have come to think of science with a big S as being all clearness and light. There is indeed a most important sense in which science stands for law and certainty.

---

* Numbers in parentheses refer to numbered items in the Bibliography at the end of the book.

Scientific laws are the basis of the staggering achievements of technology that have changed the Western world, making it, in spite of all its dangers, a more comfortable and a happier place. But if you talk to a scientist you may soon find that his ideas are not all well ordered. He loves discussion, but he does not think always with complete, consistent schemes, such as are used by philosophers, lawyers, or clergymen. Moreover, in his laboratory he does not spend much of his time thinking about scientific laws at all. He is busy with other things, trying to get some piece of apparatus to work, finding a way of measuring something more exactly, or making dissections that will show the parts of an animal or plant more clearly. You may feel that he hardly knows himself what law he is trying to prove. He is continually observing, but his work is a feeling out into the dark, as it were. When pressed to say what he is doing he may present a picture of uncertainty or doubt, even of actual confusion.

Although the methodology of the scientist may appear haphazard, there is an overall conception of the goals. Excursions into apparatus design, discussion, and other enjoyable side paths nevertheless remain within the ultimate plan of knowledge and its discovery.

There are times when the curiosity of the scientist is piqued by the unusual and the unexplained in situations that do not lend themselves easily to experimentation, but which are potential stimuli to research. Let me give you an example of one such curious situation (50). Some time ago a famous world traveler gave the following description of the planet Mars and its satellites:

They have . . . discovered two lesser stars or satellites which revolve about Mars whereof the innermost is distant from the center of the primary planet exactly three of his diameters and the outermost five; the former revolves in the space of ten hours, and the latter in twenty-one and a half; so that the squares of their periodical times are very near in the same proportion with the cubes of their distance from the center of Mars, which evidently shows them to be governed by the same law of gravitation that influences the other heavenly bodies.

This is an accurate picture of Mars. It does have two moons. The given revolutions are quite close to the actual periods. Phobos goes around Mars in the same direction that Mars rotates, but in about one-third the time. This makes it appear as though Phobos rises in the West and sets in the East. It has been noted that this is the only body in the universe that revolves around a central body faster than the latter rotates. Despite the fact that this is unique, it is in the traveler's description, and we find that it is a most accurate portrayal of Mars and the unusual nature of its satellites.

Why should this be so interesting? Because the famous world traveler who wrote this was Lemuel Gulliver in 1726 as represented by Jonathan Swift in *Gulliver's Travels*. While this was written in 1726, the two moons were not discovered until 1877, a century and a half after Gulliver's description. As a matter of fact, no telescope big enough to see the moons was built until about 1820.

This is one way research begins. How come? While this may be too colloquial for the scientific mind, it expresses the beginning of wonderment. How was Gulliver able to describe these moons so accurately 150 years before they were discovered? Is it coincidence? Is it possible that Jonathan Swift had some information which others did not have? Was it merely a good guess? We have no answer to this, but it does provide stimulation for possible investigation.

The Careful Casual

In the Preface, I suggested a fundamental law of research, rather an informal one, which states that "people don't usually do research the way people who write books about research say that people do research." This book, like so many others, primarily presents an ideal for research methodology or, perhaps, a general set of principles to guide but not to constrict a researcher.

Foremost among the qualities a good researcher needs is what Pasteur has called the prepared mind. It is clearly impossible for anyone engaged in research to predict all of the events that may occur. The researcher must begin with care in the planning and execution of his research, but he must not become so rigidly tied to the plan that he is rendered incapable of seeing accidental discoveries that may pop up, much in the way Fleming did in the example given above regarding the accidental discovery of penicillin. The researcher must be a little casual as well, for a relaxed but nevertheless alert view toward research may provide the occasion for unexpected discovery. This is what Pasteur means by the prepared mind, a combination of stored basic knowledge and a readiness to perceive the unusual.

Walter B. Cannon, in his work on the way of an investigator (35), has referred to this type of accidental discovery as "serendipity." This is a term taken from Walpole's *Three Princes of Serendip*, a story of three princes who went around the world searching for something, did not find what they were seeking, but on their journeys discovered many things that they had not sought. Cannon indicates that serendipity, or accidental discovery, is a major quality of research and the prepared mind must be alert for it.

And so the researcher must be careful and casual. Another aspect of research is the way in which it is conceived and carried out. When an article appears in a professional scientific journal, it usually follows a predetermined and generally accepted format. Most articles will begin with an introduction, a review of the literature, a description of the experimental design, a presentation of the results obtained in the experiment, a discussion of those results, and a summary, followed by a bibliography of relevant articles. Such scientific papers are usually astringent and formal and in no way truly reflect the very informal, enjoyable aspects of sitting around in a laboratory with one's colleagues and talking about the way research might be accomplished. The end product is a dehydrated form of the entire story.

One of the problems that faces us in the United States is what I refer to as a "conspiracy of efficiency." The American scientist is much less relaxed than, for example, his British counterpart. The journals make the research look exceptionally organized with its inevitable progress from title to bibliography. This is an extremely well-organized and effective means of presenting the information,* but it is not necessarily the way research is organized.

The British are willing to allow an excursion into humor in the middle of the scientific discussion if it serves to elucidate or amuse. For example, in the middle of a discussion on rudimentary brain development British neurologist W. Grey Walter (52) interrupts the flow of his essay to introduce a bit of doggerel. He talks about a dinosaur that had two brains: "One in his head, the usual place, the other at the spinal base. Thus, he could reason *a priori*, as well as *a posteriori.*"

The choice of an audience is in itself an interesting scientific function. If professional journals become the major avenue of scientific communication, then the reports will necessarily be brief because of constraints of space. Moreover, they will assume a common background of readership. For example, a psychologist reporting a psychoanalytic study would not be likely to define Freudian terms such as "id" or "superego" because he would assume that a person reading the journal would share a common knowledge of basic concept and theory. Similarly, an operant conditioner reporting research in the

---

* It is also likely that publication costs, which have soared over the years, make a tighter presentation of the research data more efficient but infinitely much less fun.

Journal of the Experimental Analysis of Behavior would not feel it necessary to define schedules of reinforcement. There is a need for some repository of this assumed background of shared knowledge, and this need, as T. Kuhn (61) points out, is served by the scientific textbook.

The function of the textbook is "to expound the body of accepted theory, illustrate many or all of its successful applications, and compare these applications with exemplary observations and experiments" (62). The textbook, then, becomes for the scientific practitioner a statement of an agreed-upon body of theory and data, a model for his science. But it creates a problem, in that the scientist—particularly the student scientist pressed for time—tends to rely increasingly on the text as his primary source of information and rarely goes back to original sources. Why need a student read Hull or Tolman in the original when current textbooks present the theoretical positions of these men in a lucid and systematic fashion? The student interested in the *processes* underlying the developments in their theories must go to the research journals to recapture the flavor of the experimentation as the two schools advanced their somewhat competing positions. The text also presents a view of the development of a science that may appear oversimplified and selective. Science, as Kuhn observes (63), has little room for repudiated books, and "the result is a sometimes drastic distortion in the scientist's perception of his discipline's past. More than the practitioner of other creative fields, he comes to see [the past] as leading in a straight line to the discipline's present vantage."

All texts are not equivalent. If everything in a science were *fully* agreed upon, one textbook per field would suffice. Variations in textbooks (note the many introductory psychology textbooks) normally reflect differences in emphasis or style of presentation, although in fields where theoretical disagreements abound the textbook may become a salvo in a battle for the advancement of one model over another.

It is true that the textbook itself often begins to assume some shared background of specialized knowledge. Most books in science are now texts not addressed to the generally educated audience of interested laymen, which includes scientists from other disciplines.

Contrast the average textbook of today with Darwin's *Origin of Species*, which was addressed to any literate person interested in the field, without special reference to practitioners. The need today is probably served as well as anywhere in the excellent journal *Scientific American*, addressed to the intelligent layman.

For the practicing scientist the constraints of texts and journals are necessary for the advancement of his field. But for the historian and philosopher of science, as well as for those who are generally interested in the creative process, the distillation of years of thought and experimentation into the formal research report (as I have observed a number of times in this book) is a loss.

Let me give you a personal example of such an event. In research some of my associates and I were doing on verbal behavior in human subjects, we were looking for some sort of reinforcer to use as a reward for speaking. Our subjects were equipped with individual microphones and we were studying the verbal patterns of individuals and of these same individuals in group interaction. They were paid by the hour for this. But it seemed to us, as we were sitting around talking about the experiment, that this was not an adequate reward for our purposes inasmuch as it did not matter how much or how loud the subject spoke during the session. He received the same amount no matter how much he talked. So we wondered what would happen if we tried to get him to speak louder or faster by rewarding him for such verbalization. Recognizing that money is a very good reward in our culture, we decided that it would be a fine idea to see what would happen if we paid the subject in money as he was speaking, so that each impulse spoken into the microphone would be rewarded. What would happen if we paid him by the spoken impulse? We thought that a coin dropping into a chute each time he spoke above a certain amplitude would be a good reinforcer to produce and maintain such behavior.

But then we started counting up the number of such impulses during an hour session and found that there would be several hundred. It would be financially impossible to use coins unless we were to use pennies. In the course of this informal discussion, it was decided that pennies are not really very good rewards in our culture. There seems to be more than five times the rewarding value of a penny on a nickel. So the minimum successful financial reward in the form of a coin would probably be a nickel. This would become so expensive as a reward in such an experiment that if we did use the nickel the chances are the experimenters would try to change places with the subject!

Someone suggested that we might try using poker chips that the subjects could exchange for money at the end of the session. In this way they would be working for a symbolic monetary reward, which is very strongly reinforced in our culture. We talked about the meaning of poker chips and the images that poker chips conjured up in the minds of various people in a group. Stacks of poker chips in front of a gambler in a smoke-filled room and the various dramatic associations of poker chips in the folklore of our culture were discussed. Of course there was a lot of joking about this and someone wanted to know if we would have to wear green eyeshades and roll up our sleeves and put garters on them, whether we would have to use a round table for the experiment with a green felt cloth over it and so on, invoking the humor of the gambling situation. We finally decided to use chips.

The above account is merely a capsule record of the many hours of discussion on an informal level which went on during this particular part of the experiment. When the paper was finally written up for publication in professional journals, it merely reported that "because of the generalized reinforcing nature of poker chips, they were used as a reinforcement for verbal behavior as a substitute for monetary reward (but symbolic of such secondary monetary reinforcement) and to be exchanged for money." Nothing about the green eyeshade, the green felt cloth, the sleeve-garters, the smoke-filled room—remarks which would be inappropriate for a scientific paper.

But I do think that it is somewhat unfortunate that the joking and informality of group research discussions are filtered out by the time they appear in a published form. Students who might otherwise consider research as an enjoyable career are given the idea that research is a tedious, astringent, rigid discipline. In short, the careful always appears in print but rarely the casual. Where the casual does appear is in the informal contacts among scientists, both in their own laboratories and in meetings, such as conventions. If there is one important function served by a convention of scientists (who get together perhaps once a year), it is not the presentation of papers but the informal contacts in bars and restaurants that provide the opportunity for the exchange of ideas and information.

A Case of Serendipity

In a research report designed specifically to study examples of accidental discovery and the ways of an investigator, two sociologists, Bernard Barber and Renee Fox (12), interviewed two well-qualified research scientists, both of whom had observed an event but only one of whom had followed through to an eventual discovery. Barber and Fox call this article "The Case of the Floppy Eared Rabbits: An Instance of Serendipity Gained and Serendipity Lost." Because this is one of the most valuable examples available of accidental discovery, I would like to discuss it in some detail.

Barber and Fox had heard of a discovery two researchers had made accidentally. One of these two scientists was Dr. Lewis Thomas, an eminent scientist who, at the time of the paper (1958), was head of the Department of Medicine at New York University's College of Medicine and formerly had been Professor and Chairman of the Department of Pathology. The other researcher was Dr. Aaron Kellner, then associate professor in the Department of Pathology of Cornell University Medical College and director of its central laboratories.

Both of these scientists were well qualified, well respected, and affiliated with excellent medical schools. In the course of their research in pathology, both men had had occasion to inject rabbits with an enzyme, papain, and both of them had observed that the ears of the rabbits collapsed following the injection. Despite the fact that both of them had observed the floppy ears following the intravenous injection of the rabbits, only one of them went on to discover the explanation for this unusual and funny event. The reasons for this present a fascinating picture of the conditions under which research usually occurs and what happens to researchers.

Barber and Fox quote from interviews with both Dr. Thomas and Dr. Kellner. Let us quote from Dr. Thomas, who first noticed the reversible collapse of the rabbits' ears when he was working on the effects of a class of enzymes, proteolytic enzymes.* Dr. Thomas said (13):

I was trying to explore the notion that the cardiac and blood vessel lesions in certain hypersensitivity states may be due to release of proteolytic enzymes. It's an attractive idea on which there's little evidence. And it's been picked up at some time or another by almost everyone working on hypersensitivity. For this investigation I used trypsin, because it was the most available enzyme around the laboratory, and I got nothing. We also happened to have papain; I don't know where it had come from; but because it was there, I tried it. I also tried a third enzyme, ficin. It comes from figs, and it's commonly used. It has catholic tastes and so it's quite useful in the laboratory. So I had these three enzymes. The other two didn't produce lesions. Nor did papain. But what the

---

* Proteolytic enzymes are enzymes that by catalytic action accelerate the hydrolysis of proteins into simpler organic substances.

papain did was always produce these bizarre cosmetic changes. . . . It was one of the most uniform reactions I'd ever seen in biology. It always happened. And it looked as if something important must have happened to cause this reaction."

There are several particularly interesting phrases in this initial account of the discovery. For one thing he says "For this investigation I used trypsin, because it was the *most available enzyme around the laboratory* . . ." (italics mine). He goes on to say "we also happened to have papain; I don't know where it had come from; but because it was there, I tried it." Here, indeed, is accident. They "happened to have" one enzyme and the other was "the most available" around the laboratory. Certainly there is none of the rigorous preconceived hypothesis-testing in the choice of these particular enzymes. It was mostly accident that they "happened" to be in the lab.

Being a good research scientist, Dr. Thomas did not let this unusual event go by. He goes on (14) to describe his immediate search for an explanation:

I chased it like crazy. But I didn't do the right thing . . . I did the expected things. I had sections cut, and I had them stained by all the techniques available at the time. And I studied what I believed to be the constituents of a rabbit's ear. I looked at all the sections, but I couldn't see anything the matter. The connective tissue was intact. There was no change in the amount of elastic tissue. There was no inflammation, no tissue damage. I expected to find a great deal, because I thought we had destroyed something.

Here is another significant phrase appearing, "I did the expected things." He went on and cut the sections, and stained them by all the techniques available at the time of the experiment. He said that he "expected to find a great deal" because he thought that something had been destroyed. At that time he also indicated that he had studied the cartilage of the rabbit's ear and considered it normal. ". . . The cells were healthy-looking and there were nice nuclei. I decided there was no damage to the cartilage. And that was that . . ." He did say that his examination of the cartilage at that time was routine and fairly casual because he did not entertain the idea seriously that the collapse of the ears might be associated with cartilage change. "I hadn't thought of cartilage. You're not likely to, because it's not considered interesting . . . I know my own idea had always been that cartilage is a quiet, inactive tissue."

It is undoubtedly true that people do have preconceptions such as Dr. Thomas had. He thought that there must be some damage and found none. He assumed that the damage would be in the connective or elastic tissues of the ear and shared a conviction with others that cartilage is "inert and relatively uninteresting," so he didn't pay much attention to it. This made him unreceptive to the actual explanation for the floppy ears as changes in the cartilage. He discovered this explanation accidentally a number of years later.

Dr. Thomas was very anxious to get some explanation for this uniform biological event, but he finally was obliged to turn away from his floppy-eared rabbits because he was "terribly busy working on another problem at the time," a problem with which he was "making progress." And he also remarked that he had "already used up all the rabbits I could afford, so I was able to persuade myself to abandon this other research." Here are two other impinging events that changed the course of the research. He was doing other research in which he was making progress (rewarding to him) and his budget could not provide for the large number of rabbits he felt he needed in order to pursue this adequately. So he was able to persuade himself to abandon this other research with the floppy-eared rabbits and temporarily accept the failure.

Barber and Fox note that it is usual not to report such negative experiments in the scientific literature for many reasons, not the least of which is the lack of available space for what might be interesting and perhaps valuable experiments but ones which are not worked out as relatively complete research projects. No one else, therefore, was formally told about Dr. Thomas' work with the floppy-eared rabbits. But he did not forget them and he kept the problem of the floppy ears alive through many informal contacts with colleagues who visited his labs and through other informal meetings. For example, he noted that twice he demonstrated this phenomenon for some of his unbelieving colleagues. As he said, "They didn't believe me when I told them what happened. They didn't really believe that you can get that much change and not a trace of anything having happened when you look in the microscope." In this way, the issue remained alive by informal exchanges among scientists.

A couple of years after this accidental discovery, Dr. Thomas was doing another type of experiment. He said:

> I was looking for a way . . . to reduce the level of fibrinogen in the blood of rabbits. I had been studying a form of fibrinoid which occurs inside blood vessels in the generalized Schwartzman reaction and which seems to be derived from fibrinogen. My working hypothesis was that if I depleted the fibrinogen and, as a result, fibrinoid did not occur, this would help. It had been reported that if you inject proteolytic enzymes, this will deplete fibrinogen. So I tried to inhibit the Schwartzman reaction by injecting papain intravenously into the rabbits. It didn't work with respect to fibrinogen . . . But the same damned thing happened again to the rabbits' ears!

This time, fortunately, Dr. Thomas was able to solve this puzzle of the floppy ears and to realize that it was an instance of accidental discovery. In his words this is what happened:

> I was teaching second-year medical students in pathology. We have these small seminars with them: two-hour sessions in the morning, twice a week, with six to eight students. These are seminars devoted to experimental pathology and

the theoretical aspects of the mechanism of disease. The students have a chance to see what we, the faculty, are up to in the laboratory. I happened to have a session with the students at the same time that this thing with the rabbits' ears happened again. I thought it would be an entertaining thing to show them . . . a spectacular thing. The students were very interested in it. I explained to them that we couldn't really explain what the hell was going on here. I did this experiment on purpose for them, to see what they would think . . . Besides which, I was in irons on my other experiments. There was not much doing on those. I was not being brilliant on these other problems . . . Well, this time I did what I didn't do before. I simultaneously cut sections of the ears of rabbits after I'd given them papain and sections of normal ears. This is the part of the story I'm most ashamed of. It still makes me writhe to think of it. There was no damage to the tissue in the sense of a lesion. But what had taken place was a quantitative change in the matrix of the cartilage. The only way you could make sense of this change was simultaneously to compare sections taken from the ears of rabbits which had been injected with papain with comparable sections from the ears of rabbits of the same age and size which had not received papain . . . Before this I had always been so struck by the enormity of the change that when I didn't see something obvious, I concluded there was nothing . . . Also, I didn't have a lot of rabbits to work with before.

This is one of the major functions that students serve. They remind instructors of the way in which research should have been done originally. Because he was obliged to "do it right," in a sense, and carefully compare normal and papain-injected rabbits' ears as an example for the students, he went on to discover quantitative change in the cartilage, which was the explanation for the floppy ears. Let me quote finally from Dr. Thomas' article (from the *Journal of Experimental Medicine*) in which he reported what had happened to the cartilage in the ears of the rabbits. It is quite technical, but this is the final product of the years of informal contacts, puzzles, searching, and accident. "The ear cartilage showed loss of a major portion of the intercellular matrix, and complete absence of basophilia from the small amount of remaining matrix. The cartilage cells appeared somewhat larger, and rounder than normal, and lay in close contact with each other . . . (The contrast between the normal ear cartilage and tissue obtained 4 hours after injection is illustrated in Figs. 3A and 3B of this article.)" What a very formal way to report on the wonderfully human fun and bewilderment which had gone on for so many years in Dr. Thomas' laboratory!

One final interesting accidental discovery was made when Dr. Thomas was demonstrating to students (16).

I was so completely sold on the uniformity of this thing that I used the same rabbit (for each seminar). . . . The third time it didn't work. I was appalled by it. The students were there, and the rabbit's ears were still in place. . . . At first I thought that perhaps the technician had given him the wrong stuff. But then when I checked on that and gave the same stuff to the other rabbits and it *did* work I realized that the rabbit had become immune. This is a potentially hot finding. . . .

This is the train of accident and discovery followed by Dr. Thomas. Dr. Kellner, an equally qualified scientist, saw the floppy-eared rabbits when he was working with injections of papain but did not go on to make the discovery, primarily because the train of discovery led him elsewhere. First of all, Dr. Kellner was interested in muscle tissue and cardiac research. When he observed the changes in the rabbits' ears during some research on heart muscle he said he was "a little curious about it at the time" and "followed it up to the extent of making sections of the rabbits' ears." Here his interest in muscle and his preconceived ideas about cartilage (the same as Dr. Thomas —the inert quality) kept him from seeing further (17):

Since I was primarily interested in research questions having to do with the muscles of the heart, I was thinking in
terms of muscle. That blinded me, so that changes in the
cartilage didn't occur to me as a possibility. I was looking
for muscles in the sections, and I never dreamed it was
cartilage.

One major influence on Dr. Kellner was the people associated
with him in the laboratory, research colleagues who shared his
interest in cardiac muscle and who reinforced his tendency to
move away from the amusing puzzle of the floppy ears to other
areas closer to everyone's interest. There were also some
serendipitous discoveries attendant upon the floppy ears. Among
other things, Dr. Kellner was able to discover a blood coagula-
tion defect in papain-injected rabbits, a defect which resembled
hemophilia in certain respects. So it is possible that serendipity
here, while it did not lead to the cartilage explanation of the
floppy ears, might lead to other eventual findings of critical
importance.

Preconceived Ideas: Hypothesis Myopia

On page 59 we will begin a more formal discussion on hypothesis-testing and theory in science, but it seems appropriate
at this point to comment on *hypothesis myopia*, a common
disease among researchers holding certain preconceived ideas
that might get in the way of discovery. We have seen this illustrated in the case of two eminent scientists, Drs. Thomas and
Kellner, both of whom were delayed in a discovery by a preconceived idea about the inert nature of cartilage. But these researchers missed a point only because they did not immediately
go on to find some new facts. What I choose to call hypothesis
myopia is a disorder of vision, a research nearsightedness in
which the sufferer has the facts clearly in view and, because of
preconceived notions, either refuses to accept them or at-

tempts to explain them away. Let me give you two well-documented cases of hypothesis myopia, one reported during the time of Galileo and the other a more recent case.

Galileo, in looking through his newly invented telescope, discovered that there were spots on the sun. He presented these findings to his colleagues and one group, followers of an Aristotelian mode of thought, rejected his data. Their theory of the composition of celestial matter indicated to them that the sun could not possibly have spots, and so they refused to look through his telescope! Their argument in this was simple: the sun had no spots; if the telescope showed spots on the sun, then the telescope was distorting the perception. Inasmuch as they knew there were no spots, why should they bother to look through an obviously erroneous instrument?

There is some merit in one phase of that argument—the reliability of the instrument. A first step in such research would have to be a check of the reliability of the telescope and, in part, the Aristotelians were correct in questioning its accuracy. But they were myopic in refusing to make such a check (which could easily be done in a testable earth situation) and in refusing to allow any question of their "certain knowledge" of the lack of spots on the sun.

The second is a mild case of hypothesis myopia involving two physicists who performed a carefully devised experiment and obtained negative results.

In 1887 two physicists, Albert Michelson and Edward Morley, performed an experiment to measure the exact speed of light. They built a piece of apparatus to make this exact measurement, consisting of two lengths of pipe placed at right angles to each other. One pipe was pointed in the direction of the earth's movement around the sun, while the other was pointed across the direction of the earth's motion. They then placed a mirror at the end of each pipe and one at the point of intersection. They flashed a beam of light into each pipe at precisely the same moment; this beam struck the mirror at the point of intersection, reflected down the length of the pipes, struck the mirror at each end and reflected back to the central mirror. The prevailing theory at that time was that an invisible ether filled all space that wasn't occupied by solid objects. If this theory were correct, then one ray of light would have been going against the "current" of ether while the other would be going with the current, therefore faster. But this is not what happened. The two beams of light returned to the central mirror at exactly the same moment. The results of the experiment were considered negative; that is, they failed to confirm the hypothesis that light would be slowed if the earth moved through ether. As Paul Copeland and William Bennett (40) observe, the experiment performed produced "a negative result [which] left a major problem of interpretation." Despite the evidence that light paths had wave characteristics, "previous examples of wave motion required a material medium" (as illustrated by sound in air) and it was difficult to find such a material medium for light. The conclusion of the experiment was necessarily that light was not propagated in a medium as sound is propagated in air.

Copeland and Bennett further note that G. F. FitzGerald tried to explain the negative results in terms of contraction of one of the arms of the apparatus; that is, the length of pipe pointed in the direction of the motion contracted just enough to compensate for the difference in interference. Other interpretations of the results were also couched in terms of the prevailing theory of ether. While physicists accepted the data, they were unable to fit them into the existing hypotheses until Einstein, in 1905, provided a major reconstruction of the theory in his famous paper dealing with the special theory of relativity. With regard to the "negative" results obtained by Michelson and Morley, he explained what had occurred. They had measured the speed of light accurately and the theory of the existence of ether was incorrect. He stated that light always travels at the same speed no matter what the conditions and that, moreover, the motion of the earth with regard to the sun has no effect on the speed of light. We might not expect Michelson and Morley to come up with the special theory of relativity from their data, but we can expect that when results conflict with theory they question the theory. In a very real sense, there is no such thing as a negative result or a failure in an experiment. Every datum obtained provides information to the prepared mind, which respects data and does not let hypotheses get in the way of research.

Chapter Two
Characteristics and Goals of Science

Some Important Characteristics of Science

I have already noted that science is a mixture of doubt and certainty. I think the good scientist is arrogantly humble. This isn't just a play on words; I think he should be arrogant in method and humble in his belief in his knowledge. To me, as a psychologist, this is particularly applicable. There is so much we do not know as yet in the study of behavior that a proper humility is essential, but this should never lead us to accept unscientific explanations of behavior (such as "human nature") which conflict with a forthright scientific method. It is better, as Skinner (86) has suggested, to remain without an answer than to accept an inadequate one. This is a major characteristic of science, the ability to wait for an answer combined with a continuing search for an explanation and a rejection of premature explanation. Skinner has also suggested other characteristics of science, among these the following: science is a set of attitudes, "it is a disposition to deal with the facts rather than with what someone has said about them" (87). Science rejects its own authorities when their statements conflict with the observations of natural events. *Data prevail, not men.*

Science, Skinner observes (88), "is a willingness to accept facts even when they are opposed to wishes." Science places a high premium on honesty* and incidents of altering data to

---

* "In the nineteenth century the famous French mathematician J. L. Lagrange once appeared before a learned society to explain a proof he

fit in with one's pet theory are unusual. But even accepting the honesty of an investigator, no one who is firmly committed to a point of view relishes seeing it demolished. If his own data succeed in destroying treasured beliefs, the scientist accepts the facts, even though it involves the loss of an old friend, a bosom theory. The moral here is clear: don't get involved with proving anything, let the data guide you. As Skinner says (89), "Experiments do not always come out as one expects, but the facts must stand and the expectations fall. The subject matter, not the scientist knows best."

Skinner has also noted (90) that science is more than a set of attitudes, it is also "a search for order, for uniformities, for lawful relations among the events in nature." It begins with a single, carefully observed event and proceeds eventually to the formulation of a general law.

I have mentioned that the scientist becomes arrogant about his methodology while he is humble about his data. This may create what Martin Gardner (51) has called the "pig-headed orthodoxy" of science, a dedication to dogma that he indicates is "both necessary and desirable for the health of science." This means that the scientist respects facts and the individual who advances a novel view is required to produce considerable evidence in order to gain recognition of his theories. The world is so full of people who have theories about every conceivable event that scientists could easily spend all their time listening to and refuting the majority of them. There must be some defense against this for, as Gardner observes, "science would be reduced to shambles by having to examine every new-fangled notion that came along. Clearly, working scientists have more important tasks. If someone announces that the moon is made of green cheese, the professional astronomer cannot be ex-

---

had worked out for a previously unsolved problem. No sooner had he started to read his paper than he suddenly stopped talking, frowned, then folded his papers and remarked, 'Gentlemen, I must think further about this.'" This is the self-correcting scientist. We probably could do very nicely with more paper-folders.

pected to climb down from his telescope and write a detailed refutation."

This pig-headed refusal to examine every theory advanced does make for some martyrs. Men of the caliber of Pasteur have been doubted and attacked. But it is a necessary filter to keep from clogging the wheels of science. And we have faith that ultimately the occasional theory that is correct and is refused an audience will emerge—for, as we have seen, data prevail, not men.

The Goals of Science

Ultimately, no matter what the scientific disciplines, the goal of science is the understanding and control of its subject matter. It may be easier to accept the understanding part of that pair because there are sciences that presently have no control of their subject matter as, for example, the disciplines of astronomy or geology. Astronomy has a highly developed body of knowledge allowing astronomers to describe and predict with high accuracy the movements of stars, for example, or the appearance of a comet. Mark Twain's Connecticut Yankee might have startled and impressed King Arthur's court by predicting an eclipse, but this is now accepted as a commonplace type of prediction. With these skills of prediction and description, astronomy still has no way of controlling celestial events; therefore, it may be said that astronomy is a descriptive science. It may further be said that astronomy will be a "pure" science when it does gain control over eclipses and comets; but this is somewhat tangential, although in recent years an experimental geology (18) has been developed, moving the descriptive science of geology closer to an experimental one.

I have brought into the goal of science two other aspects related to the goals of *understanding* and *control*—these are *description* and *prediction*, and the first of these is description. For underlying every science is observation and measurement, providing a description of events and a way of quantifying them so that experimental manipulation may be achieved. It might be said that the two critical foundations of science are *observation* and *experiment* and that *measurement* provides a meaningful way in which events and their manipulation may be ordered. The ultimate goal in science is, of course, an ordering of facts into general, consistent laws from which predictions may be made, but it inevitably starts with observation. I would like to discuss observation and experiment briefly, then the use of measurement and finally, the ordering of observation and experimental facts into general laws.

Observation and Experiment

Science is always a balance of observation and experiment, for observation is the empirical gathering of facts and experiment is the active reasoning about these facts and the manipulation of them for further knowledge. It also involves further observation under the controlled experimental condition. It has been said by students of science that Descartes and Bacon represent opposites in an approach to scientific activity. Descartes did all his work in bed, but Bacon is said to have died at the age of sixty-five from a cold that he contracted while he was experimenting in a snow drift. For Descartes, it was possible to obtain the two elements of fact and reason—which are crucial in science—without experimentation, yet this is generally not the way science advances. Reason is extended in experimentation but is rooted in observation.

Jacob Bronowski (25) has observed that science is a way of describing reality and "is therefore limited by limits of observation, and it asserts nothing which is outside of observation. Anything else is not science—it is scholastics." Here Bronowski is invoking the image of scholasticism, the philosophy of medieval Western Europe which was essentially antiempirical and certainly antiexperimental in the modern sense. But when he says that science is limited by limits of observation, he is stating one of the boundaries of scientific methodology. When he says that science asserts nothing that is outside of observation, he is again stating a basic tenet of scientific method. The observable is the very keystone of science. Einstein suggested that the fundamental unit in physics was *event—signal—observer.* By this he meant that when an event occurs it presents some outward manifestation and requires an observer to record it. Certainly this triad of event—signal—observer is basic to sciences other than physics, and it is the responsibility of the scientist, no matter what discipline he works in, carefully to observe the signal that represents the event and accurately to record it. It is for this reason that instrumentation develops. It has been said that man is between an atom and a star and has developed the microscope and the telescope to extend his views in both directions. The main purposes that an instrument serves are to provide accurate observation to eliminate observer bias and to extend and quantify the observations of the human researcher.

Now there are certainly problems in observation and in any discussion of the observer. It is important to refer to Werner Heisenberg, a German physicist who in 1927 stated the Uncertainty (or Indeterminacy) Principle, which held that it was not possible to determine at the same time both the position and speed of an electron. The observer must observe one or the other event. If he chooses to observe the position of the electron with complete accuracy, then he must relinquish an accurate evaluation of its speed and, conversely, if he wishes to study the velocity, he cannot observe its position with accuracy.* The Uncertainty Principle has come to mean that to study an event the observer must interfere with its natural course. As a result, the scientist cannot have all the relevant

---

* This, as Henry Margenau (65) points out, is not entirely correct. He says that we now have the techniques by which it would be possible to make such measurements but that these measurements would not be very meaningful overall.

information he requires at the same time. This, of course, has been taken into account in research and is really at the basis of repeated experiments in which different variables are studied in isolation. In psychology, the Uncertainty Principle has been invoked in discussions of such things as introspection, because it is not truly possible to look at oneself with clarity.

To return to Bronowski's statement that anything outside observation is not science, I would like to elaborate on this from my own point of view to say that one of the critical requirements of observation is that it be *replicable;* that is, reported by others who also are able to see and record it. This is what is meant by a data language in science. A simple example would be a physicist's pointer readings, where one observer can report an alteration in the pointer on a meter and have this observation repeated by others. The more accurate the measurement, the closer the replication of observation can be. One of the basic problems in psychology has been the lack of a universal data language to which observations may be related and in which observations may be expressed. It is obviously different, for instance, to talk about a disordered personality and a deflection in a needle of three degrees. The margin of error in the former description is great, while in the latter it is minimal. Psychology's need for a data language to sharpen observation has been considered by Joel Greenspoon (53) and R. C. Davis (42), both of whom suggest physical referents for psychological observation and description. The data language of psychology will be discussed in a bit more detail in the section on operational methods, beginning on page 74.

I suggest, then, that if the observation is not clear or replicable within the limits of observation defined, then it is not liable to scientific study. It may become so in the future when instrumentation enlarges the ability to measure and observe, but this in no way changes the criterion for scientific boundaries. As we saw in discussing characteristics of science, it is better to wait for an answer than to create an inadequate one.

There are many areas of study that may be approached experimentally, using all the sophisticated statistical and design techniques available to science, yet still remain outside the realm of scientific investigation. One of these, singled out because it illustrates many of the things I wish to bring out, is the area of parapsychology, the study of paranormal events, such as telepathy and extrasensory perception (ESP). There is no doubt that there are investigators in parapsychology who are diligent, industrious, and creative. At the moment, however, despite the use of scientific tools such as experimental design and statistical proof, there are factors that place parapsychology beyond science. One of these is the problem of observer replicability. For example, the failure of one investigator to achieve results with a particular experimental subject while another investigator apparently gets good results in terms of high scoring on extrasensory perception tasks has been explained as a problem in attitude. An experimenter who is hostile to the hypothesis of extrasensory perception will not get good results, while a sympathetic experimenter will. The assumption (as yet unproved) is that these attitudes in some way affect the mental activity of the subject.

Even though it may sound unnecessarily restrictive, it must be said that the data of parapsychology cannot be admitted as scientific data until the observations are consistent from experimenter to experimenter under specified conditions and with control of the variables. This does not condemn such data to a limbo from which they cannot return. It simply means that Bronowski's observation about the nonscientific character of events outside of observation must be kept in view in evaluating such research, even though the experiments are carefully conceived and executed.

Parapsychology is not alone in suffering from the problem of observer replication. Many areas of psychology labor under this handicap, largely, as I have said, because there is no clear data language that would allow for (or create) observer agreement. So parapsychology gets different results from subjects under different experimental conditions and with different experimenters. This variability of performance, while regrettable, is not unusual. What seems to exclude parapsychology from the body of science is its initial assumption of *para*normal events, illustrated in the word *extra*sensory perception. The initial assumption is that the data of parapsychology start outside normal events, and investigation has always been directed by this assumption. Science starts with the basic statement that events in nature (including behavior) are ordered and lawful and that the goal of a scientist is the search for order and similarity.

I feel (and this is obviously my own predilection) that the study of telepathy could legitimately start with a more intensive study of normal perception and not with an initial statement of the paranormal. Even the most dedicated spiritualist dealing with departed souls uses physical avenues of sight and hearing to conjure up spirits. Do people report visions? Very well. Start with a thorough examination of the normal perception of such individuals. If the horizons are extended to study visions seen across space and time, so be it, as long as you have begun with a search for order and as long as you have not ignored the most economical of explanations. The person who offers an explanation dramatically outside the current body of law in a science has the burden of proof. No one can expect a scientist to accept evidence for the reincarnation of souls without scientifically obtained proof, and this does not mean anecdotes about ghosts or previous existences. The difficulties encountered in approaching such problems scientifically are illustrated by an essay on the fate of the "deceased personality" and reincarnation (94). Such reports are observations couched in a data language difficult to subsume under standard methodologies, although so were Einstein's original formulations about space and time, at first. The obvious difference is that Einstein's observations have been validated.

To follow the hypotheses it is imperative that the experimental methodologies and apparatus be proper and appropriate.

A few years ago dramatic accounts of people who could read with their fingertips while blindfolded appeared in the United States and Russia. In these accounts individuals were given materials such as newspapers, which they were able to "see" with their fingers. A twenty-two-year-old Russian girl read print by moving a fingertip over the lines, and in the United States a young woman while blindfolded identified the colors of test cards and bits of cloth simply by rubbing them with her fingers. These accounts were indeed sensational; they gave rise to an article in the *New York Times Magazine* in March 1964 entitled "We Have More Than Five Senses." A "mentalist" appeared on television and at civic club meetings in Phoenix, Arizona, demonstrating his ability to read, while blindfolded, such items as the serial numbers on dollar bills. All of these professed abilities seem interesting and certainly deserve to be studied and explained. But the first step is to examine the control over the normal senses. In this regard, control of the experimental methodology appears to have been nonexistent.

Martin Gardner (49), in an incisive article on perception with the fingertips (referred to as dermo-optical perception, or DOP), indicates quite clearly that it is virtually impossible to put a blindfold on an individual (particularly an experienced person) and prevent a line of vision down the sides of the nose. In his article, subtitled "A Peek Down the Nose," he reports on the technique used by magicians who, while pretending to concentrate, raise their heads slightly and peek down the nose through two tiny apertures that allow them to see. They often hold the bridge of the nose between their fingers while "concentrating" for further manipulation of the blindfold. The very structure of the human face, of the cheekbones in particular, makes it impossible to obtain a perfect seal using a blindfold. As Gardner indicates, any experienced person can achieve enough of an aperture to be able to see despite putty, gauze, bandages, or any other technique used to blindfold. For an apparatus that effectively blindfolds, Gardner suggests an aluminum box with airholes at the top and a shoulder harness resting so that the individual cannot peek down his nose. Regarding "reading" by fingertips, when adequate precautions were taken (which meant more than the simple type of blindfold mask used), the results were negative.

The same methodological problem may appear in the use of extrasensory perception (ESP) cards. These have been used to demonstrate extrasensory powers in individuals who could "read" them without normal sensory inputs. The popular set developed at Duke University consisted of five symbols: a cross, a star, a square, a circle, and waves. N. H. Pronko (68) demonstrated that with training he could have students read the cards, since, in the proper light, the embossing of the symbols appeared faintly on the backs.

Such methodology leaves us with no information as to whether it is indeed possible for individuals to read with their fingertips or through extrasensory powers. Correctly designed experiments are crucial to answering important problems and questions such as these. Although parapsychologists are perfectly correct in asking for acceptance of demonstrated experimentation, the body of science is also correct in demanding that this experimentation be accurate, appropriate, and rigorous.

A major difficulty posed by parapsychology is its acceptance of a dualistic position, which separates it completely from the natural sciences. I have no intention of getting involved in a rehash of the mind-body problem at this point—the book is too short for that—but I will state that psychology, as a science, must accept the monistic position of science and reject the temptation to deal with mental events as though they existed separately from physical ones. The main reason is simply that this position has proved successful in other sciences and fits into the search for order and uniformity basic to scientific methodology. To establish a second realm of the mental confounds the science. The argument that there are obviously mental events—such as thought processes and dreams—again confounds the issue, because the study of these events must proceed along lines established in science. The interested student may pursue this monistic line further in Joel Greenspoon (53) and Gilbert Ryle (74).

This position of rejecting observations lying outside scientific boundaries may seem narrow and harsh but, again, the burden of proof is on the person presenting such observations. This often creates a martyr to scientific rigidity (such as Pasteur or Koch or Semmelweiss) but ultimately, as we have seen, data prevail, not men. Sometimes the martyr presents a reasoned and reasonable case, as in the following quotation: "To me truth is precious . . . I should rather be right and stand alone than to run with the multitude and be wrong . . . The holding of views herein set forth has already won for me the scorn and contempt and ridicule of some of my fellowmen. I am looked upon as being odd, strange, peculiar . . . But truth is truth and though all the world reject it and turn against me, I will cling to truth still." These impressive and brave sentences are taken from a book by Charles de Ford (44) published in 1931 in which he proves the earth is flat. The statement from Gardner, quoted on page 37, about the necessary pig-headed orthodoxy of science cannot be better illustrated than by this quotation from de Ford. If his information differs from the ordered information of the relevant science, then his responsibility is to offer proof. And science's responsibility is to listen.

Reason from Experiment: Toward Order and Law

The first step in scientific method, then, is observation or the empirical gathering of facts. But facts themselves are not enough. They are merely the first step. As I have mentioned, ordering through reasoned activity is essential to the achievement of the ultimate goals of science. Science is by no means merely a collection of isolated facts, no matter how accurately they have been observed and recorded. It is the search for consistency or order within the facts that characterizes the scientific method.* To record X and Y and Z accurately is indeed the critical first step, but science eventually has to describe the similarities existing among variables and their functional relationship. As Bronowski has observed (26) ". . . the truth of science is not truth to fact, which can never be more than approximate, but the truth of the laws which we see within the facts."

The scientist moves from the careful observation of events to a search for order, for consistencies and uniformities, for functional, lawful relationships among the events that he has studied. Beginning with a single isolated event, he attempts to find more and more information that will relate events in some meaningful and consistent order. He requires uniformity of events. Bronowski elsewhere has said (27):

We cannot define truth in science until we move from fact to law. And within the body of laws in turn, what impresses us as truth is the orderly coherence of the pieces. They fit together like the characters in a great novel, or like the words in a poem. Indeed, we should keep that last analogy by us always. For science is language and, like a language, it defines its parts by the way they make up a meaning. Every word in the sentence has some uncertainty of definition, and yet the sentence defines its own meaning and that of its words conclusively. It is the eternal unity and coherence of science which give it truth, and which make it a better system of prediction than any less orderly language.

In this sense, science becomes a language, as Bronowski has

---

* In 1848, Renan (73) wrote in *L'Avenir de la Science* (*The Future of Science*): "All the special sciences start by the affirmation of unity, and only begin to distinguish when analysis has revealed numerous differences where before had been visible nothing but uniformity. Read the Scottish psychologists, and you will find at each page that the primary rule of the philosophical method is to maintain distinct that which is distinct, not to anticipate facts by a hurried reduction to unity, not to recoil before the multiplicity of causes."

suggested, for describing nature. It begins with a statement of faith and assumption that the world is orderly, that the events in the world are lawful and understandable. This is no less true of psychology and the study of behavior than it is of the study of physics or chemistry. A psychologist cannot function effectively as a scientist unless he accepts the assumption that behavior is lawful and understandable, recognizing also the somewhat chilling fact that the scientific goal is control of behavior. Later on, when we talk about ethical considerations in research, we will discuss some of the problems of ethics in the control of behavior. At the moment I need only observe that psychology, as a scientific discipline, accepts the general tenet of the lawfulness and uniformity of natural events, a tenet that every other science has discovered to be a critical foundation.

And so observation has taken us to experimentation, and experimentation has taken us to the search for order and uniformity upon which we may base laws. Sidman has offered an interesting account of a personal experience which illustrates the importance of uniformities in scientific methodology. He writes (75):

As a young graduate student . . . I felt that my work had to be different, that it had to produce something new that would startle the world. Along these lines I once wrote a paper, describing some of my work in which I emphasized how different my experiments were from anything else that had ever been done. One of my teachers, W. N. Schoenfeld, agreed that the data were very interesting. But he went on to add that I had written the paper from a peculiar point of view. I had emphasized the *differences* between my work and everyone else's. But science does not ordinarily advance that way. It is the job of science to find orderly relations among phenomena, not differences. It would have been more useful if I could have pointed out the similarities between my work and previous experiments.

This does not mean, by any stretch of the imagination, that scientists are attempting to conform. Nor are they merely trying to repeat the experiments of others, or question experimental data that others may have achieved. Far from it. It means simply that the more we can develop likenesses and orderly relationships among events, the closer we are to effective prediction and control of our science. When we discover, for example, the likenesses that exist between the baccillus, the virus, and the crystal, or the functional similarities that may exist between the cell and the organism and society, we move closer to effective prediction.

Prediction from Observation and Experiment

I have noted that science is a technique for ordering events into lawful relationships, and that the goal of science is prediction and control based on such lawfulness. A law, as it is usually described, is a collection of facts grouped into a consistent body of knowledge, from which it is possible to make predictions. But it is obvious that no prediction is completely certain because it is not possible to know all the variables operating in a particular situation. All we ask of a prediction is that it be based on a lawful ordering of events and that it forecast, as accurately as possible, what will happen in a future event within a range of uncertainty.

This introduces the basic concept of *probability*, which is fundamental to scientific method. We talk about the probabilities of an event occurring. We are, in a sense, giving odds, saying the chances are that if X is manipulated in a certain fashion, Y will change in a certain way. Experimentation is clearly a method for increasing the likelihood of the prediction being correct.

Let's take a simple example of this. If you were to observe a dog drinking water, you would be likely to say that the dog was thirsty, inferring from past experience that a dog lapping up water has been deprived of water and is thirsty. This is a probable inference and in all likelihood a pretty good guess. Although this explanation is the most probable account of his behavior, it is also possible that other factors might have played a role. For example, a bee might have landed on his tongue, or some cayenne pepper, or perhaps he was after a piece of meat at the bottom of the bucket. These are all unlikely events in terms of frequency of occurrence, and so we base our interpretation of the dog's thirst on past experience. If we wished to increase the probability of our explanation being the correct one, we would experiment. We would take the dog and keep him in an enclosure for forty-eight hours without water. At the end of that time, we could provide food and water and see how active his drinking behavior might be. Assuming that depriving him had produced a tissue need for water and increased the likelihood of drinking, we could now place more confidence in deprivation as a critical variable in drinking behavior. With this established, we could return to our earlier explanations of the dog's behavior with added information and confidence.

It must be kept in mind that there is always an element of uncertainty in a prediction. The scientist must always be seeking methods of improving the accuracy of his predictions. This is essentially what we mean when we talk about controlling events. It is interesting to note that in the area of prediction some people, who ordinarily accept the basic principles of science such as accurate observation, description, and experiment, feel that we have entered into a never-never land. Sir Oliver Lodge, for example, observed: "Though an astronomer can calculate the orbit of a planet or comet or even a meteor, although a physicist can deal with the structure of atoms, and a chemist with their possible combinations, neither a biologist nor any scientific man can calculate the orbit of a common fly." Now, with all respect to Sir Oliver, this is rather a nonsensical statement. For one thing, who could ever say that it is impossible to accomplish something? Only a nearsighted or pessimistic person could assume that the observations or measurements currently unavailable to us will always remain beyond our reach. A careful reading of Sir Oliver's high-sounding statement should bring to mind one question. Who has *tried* to calculate the orbit of a common fly?

I am certain that if it were important enough to have such a calculation, steps could be taken to try to measure it. Let us play for a moment with this speculation, because it is one that seems to hit at the center of some of the assumptions we have made. We assume that behavior is lawful and, therefore, if we are true to our own beliefs, the orbit of a fly in, say, a cathedral should be understandable, provided we had sufficient information about the organism and the environment in which it is behaving. How would we proceed to get pertinent information to predict the orbit of this particular fly? Perhaps we might start with an examination of air currents in the cathedral. Suppose we were to divide the cathedral into a grid and, in making accurate observations and measurements, learn that at point B-6, which is 30 feet from the floor and 25 feet from the west wall, there is a strong draft that provides a considerable amount of resistance to any object caught in that coordinate. We might assume that a fly would be less likely to fly into a resistance area, which would be pushing against his flight, than one offering less of an obstacle. This may be completely wrong, but at least it may be the beginning of a calculation of an orbit. It might, upon further investigation, appear that temperature changes may be a critical variable. Certainly this seems to be true in calculating the migration of birds or spawning behavior in salmon, which Sir Oliver might have also considered beyond the ken of the scientist. In addition, there may be organismic variables such as the presence of lady flies, the strength of the fly, the length of time since his last meal, and others which might prove relevant.

I certainly have no intention of plotting coordinates to test out the idea that it may be possible to predict the orbit of a fly in a cathedral, but I feel sure that if this should become something of importance in science, someone could work out a means of making such a prediction. We can simply offer our respect to Sir Oliver and ignore him in this context.

So far I have touched upon the elements of *observation, experiment*, and *prediction* as they relate to scientific method and the ultimate goals of understanding, prediction, and control. But I have not spent much time on the problem of control itself. It should be apparent that once we are able successfully to predict events, we have achieved a degree of control over them. I'll be coming back to this later on in discussing experimental manipulation. At the moment, I would like to go back to the other basic element in the beginnings of a science, the one that, coupled with observation, underlies all science, descriptive or experimental. This is the question of measurement.

Measurement in Science

In discussing the question of description in scientific method-ology, I have used a number of examples covering such differing events as a virus, a fly, and a dog. There are, to be sure, dif-ferent levels of description in science, ranging from description of cellular activity in a human to description of this same human courting his girl friend. The narrower the focus of activity, the easier it is to measure. For example, a scientist might be infinitely more accurate in describing electrical activity occur-ring in a person's cell membrane than he would be in describ-ing dating behavior. There are enormously complicated problem areas, such as tensions that lead to war and racial and religious prejudice, which we have been relatively unable to solve. We have not been able to solve them in large measure because they cannot be effectively described. In viewing such significant problem areas, I agree with B. J. Underwood (97) who observed: "I would defend the proposition that research in psychology necessarily involves measurement, and that the rapidity with which research will embrace . . . significant behaviors depends upon our ability to break them down into relevant parts which can be measured." One cannot, for example, measure prejudice, which is only a general term for a large number of activities.

However, one can begin to break prejudice down into its relevant parts by cataloguing the number of country clubs, housing developments, hotels, and restaurants in a particular community that, despite legal sanctions, execute policies and practices that exclude or limit participation by minority-group members. Or, one can assess the percentage of blacks and women in high-level administrative positions in universities or government. Assuming equal qualifications, a disproportionately low number of such persons in these posts would suggest the possibility of discrimination against them. Finally, the attitudes of people toward long-haired youth (a rematch of the battle between the Cavaliers and Cromwell's Roundheads?) can be assessed by studying dress codes in schools or the policy of a famous West Coast amusement park to refuse admittance (probably illegally) to persons with long hair. These are only beginnings of measurement of complex sets of behaviors, but they are nonetheless beginnings.

The two basic questions in measurement are (1) *does the phenomenon exist*? and (2) if it exists, *to what extent does it exist*? As these questions are posed in scientific terms, the first is a *nominal* type of measurement. As the term nominal suggests, this is a naming operation which simply differentiates one event from another. It is a frequent basis of measurement description. For example, classification of flowers or birds is a nominal operation. But let's see where this might lead.

To take another illustration, numbering prisoners in a penitentiary is nominal. This basic classification may be sufficient for the needs of the prison authorities, but it is possible that they may wish to separate the prisoners into groups based on an estimate of the severity of the crime for which they were imprisoned. Assuming that forgery is a less serious crime than murder, Prisoner No. 400-097 (a forger) is placed in a different cell block from Prisoner No. 400-789 (a murderer). The numbers differentiate the two on a nominal scale, the separation in terms of severity of crime differentiates them on an *ordinal* scale. It is apparent that an ordinal scale, such as a rating of severity of criminal acts, can be highly subjective. Suppose it were possible to work out an exact scale of severity so that the interval murder ↔ forgery was equal in severity to the interval forgery ↔ shoplifting. In terms of increasing seriousness of crime the ordinal scale would read: shoplifting—forgery—murder. If such a scale worked, it might be used by a judge in determining sentences, or by a parole board in assessing release of prisoners. When an ordinal scale is divided into equal steps or gradations of such changes in intensity, it is referred to as an *equal interval* scale. A final development in scaling would be one in which it were possible to establish an absolute zero point on the scale. An equal interval scale with an absolute zero point is called a *ratio* scale.

At this point I would like to express an opinion that may well meet with some disagreement. I would say that ultimately all measurements must have some physical referent (see page 75). There are phenomena that are called subjective, but if they cannot eventually lead to measurement, they cannot be considered as scientific data. This does not make a shrine out of the methods or techniques used by physics and the other sciences, but indicates that until subjective phenomena are rendered measurable and quantifiable, they can yield little meaningful information. I believe that research problems such as those of anxiety and emotion, which have always been matters of concern for psychologists, may be most fruitful when approached in terms of physiological change and a measurement of such physiological change. As we will see in Chapter 4, there have been many definitions of emotion. But the one factor common to all of these definitions is some change in the activity of the autonomic nervous system, a physiological event that is subject to measurement. In recent years, covert behavior—which has often been referred to as unconscious and presumably not subject to experimental investigation—has been studied in a careful and ingenious fashion by Ralph Hefferline and his colleagues (55). There is clear indication of the possibility of measuring minute behavioral events with physiological recordings.

It has always been true that the information available to a scientist is largely dependent upon the refinement of his instruments. Each year, as finer and finer instruments are made available to the researcher, more and more information previously considered subjective comes under the scrutiny of the experimental investigation. One of the ways measurement begins is through the use of physical or mathematical representations of objects or events. I have already mentioned the use of degrees of temperature to measure gradations of hot and cold. We have come to accept a thermometer as a reliable indication of gradations of temperature.

It may be interesting to refresh your memory as to the origins of the ever-present and reliable thermometer. Before the seventeenth century, a nominal type of measurement was considered sufficient for evaluating cold and warm. It seemed sufficient to say that something was hot or cold, or to use some very gross ordinal scale of ordering by saying "it is colder" or "it is warmer." As Isaac Asimov (2) has observed, "to subject temperature to quantitative measure, it was first necessary to find some measurable change that seemed to take place uniformly with change in temperature. One such change was found in the fact that substances expand when warmed and contract when cooled." He goes on to discuss the research of Galileo in 1603, who first tried to make use of the fact that substances expand when warmed and contract when cooled by inserting a tube of air which had been heated into a bowl of water. As the air contained in the tube began to cool to the temperature of the room, it contracted and drew water up into the tube, creating the first thermometer. When the temperature of the room changed, the level of water in the tube also changed. "If the room warmed, the air in the tube expanded and pushed the water level down; if it grew cooler, the water contracted and the water level moved up. The only trouble was that the basin of water into which the tube had been inserted was open to the air and the air pressure kept changing. That also shoved the water level up and down, independently of temperature, confusing the results."

As Asimov notes (2), the Duke of Tuscany in 1654 worked out a thermometer that was independent of air pressure, containing a liquid sealed into a bulb to which was attached a straight tube. "The contraction and the expansion of the liquid itself was used as the indication of temperature change. Liquids change their volume with temperature much less than gases do, but by using a sizeable reservoir of liquid and a filled bulb, so that the liquid could expand only up a very narrow tube, the rise and fall within that tube, for even tiny volume changes, could be made considerable." Boyle did a similar experiment about the same time as the Grand Duke of Tuscany and had shown that the human body maintained a constant temperature which was much higher than the usual room temperature. Water and alcohol were the first liquids used in the creation of thermometers, but water tended to freeze and alcohol boiled away. So the French physicist Amontons tried mercury. In Amontons' thermometer (as in Galileo's), the expansion and contraction of air produced a rise or fall in the level of the mercury. It was in 1714 that Fahrenheit combined the work of the Grand Duke of Tuscany and that of Amontons by enclosing mercury in a tube and using its own expansion and contraction with temperature as the indicator. Moreover, Fahrenheit made the contribution of putting a graded scale on his mercury tube so that the temperature might be read quantitatively. No one is quite sure as to the method by which Fahrenheit arrived at the particular scale he used on his thermometer. One account has it that he set zero at the lowest temperature he could obtain in his laboratory by mixing salt and melting ice, then setting the freezing point of clear water at 32 and its boiling point at 212. Though this appears somewhat arbitrary, it was effective because it was maintained consistently.

In 1742 Celsius, a Swedish astronomer, adopted a different scale. As it was finally developed, the freezing point of water was set at zero and its boiling point at 100 rather than the 32 and 212 of Fahrenheit. Because the scale was divided into a hundred gradations, it has been called the "centigrade" scale. The difference between the Fahrenheit and centigrade scales has continued to plague students who try to remember whether it's five-ninths plus 32 or nine-fifths plus 32 from Fahrenheit to centigrade. Because the centigrade scale (or, as it's known among many scientists, the Celsius scale) is more convenient, fitting in with the metrical system, it is used more widely among scientific persons, although the Fahrenheit scale is most popular in the United States in nonscientific measurements of temperature.

Referring back to our original notes about models, a thermometer, no matter what scale of temperature may be used, represents a physical model of contraction and expansion of a physical entity and is a reflection of changes in the environment. Later on, in Chapter 4, I will talk a little bit more about the use of physical operations in definition. At the moment, I would like to comment on one more physical model that is used as a means of measurement in our approach to ordering the data of our world. This is the model of a clock, a device that attempts to duplicate the apparent rhythmic movement of the sun. From this fundamental model of movement, the change in position of a clock's hands are taken to signify a passage of time designated by such terms as seconds, minutes and hours. In a broad sense, it may be possible to begin a consideration of time by the nominal scale, such as the binary division of day/night, late/early, and so on, moving then to gradations of lateness or earliness or dayness or nightness. The gradations then are marked off in terms of units of time, ultimately duplicating the measurements inherent in the apparent movement of the sun.

Not all models are intended to be such clearcut physical duplications of other physical operations. When one talks of the brain as a computer or of a computer as a giant brain, all that is intended is to illustrate the similarity in the information-storing and -retrieval processes going on in brains and computers. Nevertheless, whether it be by analogue or model or in the form of a conceptual system, ultimately measurement must have a base in a physical operation, or it becomes pure sophistry.

Chapter Three
Two Fundamental Methods of Research: The Formal Theoretical and the Informal Theoretical

It is time now to consider the use (and nonuse) of theory in research. So far we have touched upon methodology and have skirted around the problems of hypothesis formation and testing.

By far the predominant methodology in science is the formal theoretical approach, involving the technique of observation (an empirical one), hypothesis formulation and testing (through experimentation), and theory construction, leading to laws. Most people equate scientific method with such an approach. There is, however, another school of thought, which holds that data and not hypotheses are the stuff of science and, moreover, that theory construction need not stand in the way of investigation.

Let's take each of these approaches in turn, first the traditional, theory construction method, then the informal theoretical, recognizing that no matter what methodological differences may appear on the surface, the goal of science remains: description, explanation, prediction, and control.

Data, Hypothesis, Theory, and Law: The Formal Theoretical Method

Basic to scientific method is observation, and all research begins with it. A researcher observes an event, wonders about it, formulates some tentative ideas about it, and sets out to test the accuracy of his ideas. These are the main elements: observation–hypothesis–experiment–verification. Students of theory construction characteristically use three different sets of operations, or propositions, in evaluating theory. These are:

1. *empirical propositions* which are statements of fact, what the observer has seen.
2. *hypothetical propositions* which are statements of conjecture. Based on the observer's empirical proposition, he formulates an hypothesis to account for the observed event to be tested in experiment.
3. *theoretical propositions* which are statements of the functional relationships among variables.

Melvin Marx (66) has observed:

It is the hypothetical type of verbal proposition that forms the link between the empirical propositions, or facts, and the theories. The implications of a theory can be tested only by means of scientific predictions, or experimental hypotheses. These are questions which must be answered empirically. The hypothesis is thus the backbone of all scientific-theory construction; without it confirmation or rejection of theories would be impossible. Establishment of empirical propositions is referred to as *inductive* in contrast with the complementary development of the logical implications of theories, or the *deductive* phase of scientific investigation.

Roughly, this may be limned as follows:

Observation   Empirical observation of *facts,* reported events
↓
Hypothesis   Statement of *prediction* (if X is done, then Y should result)
↓
Experiment   Test through *manipulation* of variables
↓
Results   Confirmation or refutation of hypothesis
↓
Theory   Statement of functional relationships among variables

The theoretical framework now becomes a reference for future empirical observations, hypotheses, etcetera, with theory kept as a living body of knowledge and conjecture, subject to continual modification.

It is apparent that this system is not very different from other types of decision making or problem solving. An ordinary person making a decision or solving a problem tries to get as much information as possible (in computer language he scans), evaluates this information in terms of the present situation and his past experiences (memory), decides on a course of action in which he makes a prediction (or hypothesis) that one course of action will be better than another, and following the action, verifies his hypothesis. The final operation is one of storing this experience for future reference in a feedback to memory (7) (see the figure below).

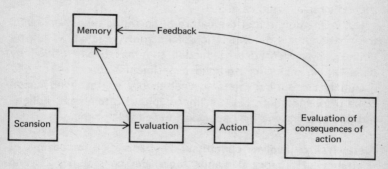

Clark Hull (56) has suggested four essentials for a sound scientific theory, which may be restated and modified as follows:

1. *Definitions and postulates.* These must be stated in an unambiguous manner; consistent with each other; or such a nature as to permit rigorous deductions.
2. *Deductions* from these postulates must be made with meticulous care, exhibited for checking in full detail. Gaps in the deductive process lead to faulty theory.
3. The significant theorems of a scientific system must take

the form of *specific statements* of the outcome of concrete experiments or observations. These predictions of outcome allow a test of the theoretical system, as we have seen in the preceding section on characteristics of theory.

4. *Carefully controlled experiments* must be devised to test the theorems deduced.

He sums up his position by observing that "Scientific theory in its best sense consists of the *strict logical deduction* from *definite postulates* of what should be *observed* under *specified conditions*. If the deductions are lacking or logically invalid, there is no theory; if the deductions involve *conditions of observation* which are *impossible of attainment,* the theory is *metaphysical* rather than scientific; . . . if the deduced phenomenon is *not observed* when the *conditions are fulfilled,* the theory is false." (Italics mine)

Hull's position is that the nature of scientific theory demands the observational determination of its truth or falsity. Truth he defines as a theoretical deduction that has been verified by observation, including rigorous experimentation.

Hull has described metaphysical theory as involving conditions of observation that are impossible of attainment. Following this thought, we may suggest the following schema:

Metaphysics: involves conditions of observation impossible of attainment. Theory demands logic and consistency but no experimental test. Religious questions would be included in this; belief in a particular body of religious ideas involves faith—acceptance of logic and consistency in the system. In general, no need is experienced for experimental proof, nor is such proof possible.

Prescience: involves deductions that are capable of being stated in terms that permit experimental verification, though no experimental tests may have yet been accomplished. Much of psychoanalytic theory might be placed here; the deductions resulting from observations may be phrased in testable hypotheses to be confirmed or refuted.

Science: involves the elements described above. Strict logical deductions from definite postulates of what should be observed under specified conditions, followed by manipulation through experimental test, rejecting false deductions.

Anatol Rapoport (70) has given some criteria for testing a theory. I have modified and enlarged upon them.

1. *The problem of definition.* Can the concepts and definitions proposed in a theory be expressed so that they may be clearly communicated to others with operational exactness?

2. *The problem of reality.* Can the effects of an event be checked by others and shown not to vary under specific circumstances, to be stable and invariant?

3. *The problem of verification.* Can the assertions made about an event be verified by experience and be subject to accurate prediction? Is the assertion true?

4. *The problem of deduction.* Does the assertion made about an event appear logical and consistent within itself and other assertions assumed to be valid, though not directly experienced? Is the assertion valid?

5. *The problem of causality.* Why did the event occur? This is one of the fundamental questions posed.

6. *The problem of communication.* Can the events and theoretical concepts be described in language (or other symbolic form) which will be clear and non-ambiguous to the receiver of the information? (This is related to Question 1.) In other words, does the terminology or other formal structure used involve vague, mutually understood but not clearly defined communication or operationally meaningful communication?

7. *The problem of parsimony.* Are the explanations economical in terms of the events described? "Occam's razor" demanded that explanations be no more involved than those which will most economically explain an event, being cer-

tain to cover all questions. In psychology, it is usually called the principle of economy in which the simplest available explanation is to be preferred.

8. *The problem of relevance.* Are assertions made about events pertinent to the whole? For example, can statements made about particular events be used to explain general behavior? As an illustration of this question, could a person talking of people in Las Vegas, Nevada, make assertions regarding all Americans? The problem of relevance is simply to determine which specific assertions are relevant to one group and which are applicable to larger wholes.

There are several points to be made about this standard theoretical orientation in science. Theory is a reasonable stage between hypothesis, experimental results, and the formulation of laws. A theory is a working model, which should be continually subjected to modification. A major objection to theory is that it may become a crystallized body of information or belief, which in itself becomes the standard for evaluating new data.* In this sense, theory becomes metaphysical and science can ill afford theories that outlast their utility as model systems. A theory begins to dominate data when a scientist becomes concerned with proving his theory to be correct at the expense of investigating the data that may or may not support it. As Ernest Renan (73) observed a century ago: "Orthodox people have as a rule very little *scientific honesty.* They do not *investigate*, they try to *prove* that this must necessarily be so. The result has been given to them beforehand; this result is true, undoubtedly true. Science has no business with it, science starts from doubt without knowing whither it is going, and gives itself up bound hand and foot to criticism which leads it wheresoever it lists."

---

* A good theory should be able to use data that fail to confirm hypotheses by modifying the theory in the light of such data.

Murray Sidman (77) sums up some of the objections to theory construction:

> What constitutes an orderly arrangement of experimental findings? Is theory the only method of organizing data? Theories themselves are subject to criteria of inclusiveness, consistency, accuracy, relevance, fruitfulness, and simplicity. They are accepted or rejected according to the number and type of phenomena they encompass, their consistency of formulation when applied to various data, the correctness of their predictions, the logical adequacy of the connections between theoretical statements and data, the number of new and interesting phenomena to which they direct attention, and the number of assumptions that are required relative to the amount of data than can be handled. It is obvious, from this list, that theory construction, while it may provide intellectual stimulation, is a hazardous occupation. This is particularly true in psychology, where the phenomena are diverse, complex, and relatively unexplored. In the face of this complexity, the current trend in psychological theorizing is toward a limited coverage of a small amount of relatively simple data.

A theory that becomes rigid is obviously not a good theory. But it is not uncommon for people to defend or attack a theory vigorously, using the same data to support conflicting interpretations.* This is all right as long as the data prevail and the

---

* In this regard it's interesting to see two investigators talking about emotion. Magda Arnold (1) in discussing recent theories of emotion, says: "The yield of the last quarter of a century has been comparatively meager. During these years a great deal of effort has been devoted to experimentation and clinical research without much concern for integrating or explaining the data." Too much data, not enough theory. Joseph Brady (23) observed, however, "In probably no other domain of psychological science has so little empirical data provided the occasion for so much theoretical speculation as in the general area of the 'emotions.'" Too much theory, not enough data. For the record, I agree with Brady.

theories remain flexible. But what happens when a theory dictates observation, when expectations of what should be in a situation override actual observations? Here is an example of this, taken from Anna Freud (48) writing about a psychoanalytic case. This was the case of a girl "in the latency period, who had succeeded in so completely repressing her envy of her little brother's penis—an affect by which her life was entirely dominated—that even in analysis it was exceptionally difficult to detect any traces of it." Now *there* is an interesting observation. It was "*exceptionally difficult to detect any traces of it,*" but theory dictated that it *should* be there. Therefore—the answer—she "*had succeeded in so completely repressing*" it, it could hardly be seen. This strikes me as a *bête noire* of theory. You cannot use the same road map every place you travel.

An interesting view of the development of a science comes from Kuhn (61), who uses the term *paradigm* to sum up significant changes in scientific theory and method. A paradigm for Kuhn is a scientific model that has two major characteristics. First, it offers a system by which events in the field can be explained better than they can be by existing models (such as Newton's *Principia*), thereby attracting a new group of adherents. Second, it is "sufficiently open-ended to leave all sorts of problems for the redefined group of practitioners to resolve." The paradigm becomes, rather than an object for replication, a model "for further articulation and speculation under new and more stringent conditions" (63). Thus the paradigm brings together a group committed to investigating it, to reevaluating existing theory and method, and to defending their findings. The group of investigators coheres in mutual experimentation. Kuhn strongly believes that the paradigm as a scientific revolution is the route to normal science, although the existence of too many models to explain events in a particular field where "competing schools . . . question each other's aims and standards" does slow scientific progress. To be sure, a science that is less mature than other sciences is more likely to have such competing schools; not long ago in psychology Hullians, Tolmanians, Skinnerians, Freudians, and others were identified as subspecies of psychologists. The lack of many competing schools in a science also contributes to an emphasis on method as opposed to theoretical positions that must be staunchly defended. Kuhn underscores methodological questions when he discusses *defining* "science," an endeavor he considers a waste of time and energy. A more reasonable question, he says (64), is: "Why does my field fail to move ahead in the way that, say, physics does? What changes in technique or method or ideology would enable it to do so?" For Kuhn another question involving a methodological emphasis is: Does a science make progress because it is a science, or does it become a science because it has made progress? How many paradigms have fallen into disuse because they did not work or because newer methodologies created new paradigms?

On page 130 we discuss resistance to change among scientists. This sort of resistance is a normal response—and necessary, unless it becomes so rigid as to prevent new looks at events. To defend existing paradigms or models in scientific enterprise is to require the proponent of a new model to demonstrate its superiority over existing models. A paradigm may meet resistance, lie fallow for a period of time, and then be rediscovered. An example of this is the model advanced by a cancer researcher a number of years ago of a paradigm for cancer based on a virological model. A virus as a factor in cancerous growth of tissue did not fit in with existing data and theory at the time; the explanation did not offer enough to require investigators to consider it as a revolutionary alternative. It was largely as a result of data coming in from other fields that a possible virological model to explain cancer was reconsidered decades after it was first stated. As a paradigm it is now a model to cohere an experimental group performing mutual study to garner the needed facts.

Kuhn also makes the point that science advances not as smooth "cumulation," but in somewhat erratic ways. Its advance depends in large measure, as we shall see, on other disciplines, on the development of ever more sophisticated methods of obtaining data and handling data analysis. Revolution and reorganization are the dominant events.

Data, Hypothesitos, Order, and Law: The Informal Theoretical Method

Adhering to the second general method of research, the informal theoretical, is a group of investigators who believe that theory construction is an uneconomical way to do research, that a researcher need only proceed from his observations to experimentation, then to some ordering of data to seek functional relationships among the variables, and finally to some formulation of organized law. Theories for this group are unnecessary because they are too formalized. These investigators consider that ordering the data and finding lawful relationships among them is the task of science, and fear that theories become solidified and begin to determine research rather than integrate research data.

Hypothesis testing is also considered to be uneconomical because the investigator working with a rigorous hypothesis feels obliged to follow it relentlessly, despite Skinner's unformalized principle of science (85) that "when you run onto something interesting, drop everything else and study it." The diligent pursuit of an hypothesis is considered by the informal theorists to be acceptable and good practice only if it does not keep you from seeing data as they begin to emerge. This group will willingly change an experiment in the middle if a new (and perhaps more promising) lead develops. They also suggest that there is no such thing as a negative result or a refutation of an hypothesis. To pursue this a bit further, investigators (such as Skinner) say that it is not good research technique to specify an hypothesis which will be confirmed or refuted. If one were to do this, they say, the confirmation of the hypothesis would provide a positive result whereas the refutation would provide a negative result. They say that there is no such thing as a negative result because any finding in an experiment is important if it provides information. Only by structuring an hypothesis in a rigorous, rigid fashion can a concept of negative results even appear. As Sidman (76) notes, "When one simply asks a question of nature, the answer is always positive."

The group of investigators who do not commit themselves to hypotheses may find some satisfaction in a famous quotation from Newton, "*Hypotheses non fingo*,"—"I do not make hypotheses." When Newton said this he meant that he derived his laws solely from observation of nature, which he thought was a process to be distinguished from formulating an hypothesis regarding the possible cause of the event observed. He also said, "I do not deal in conjectures." He believed that a careful, accurate observation of events in nature and a step-by-step pursuit* of these events would ultimately provide the material out of which a theory would evolve. A theory for Newton, and for us as well, would be some systematic formulation of the relationships among events. It is, of course, not entirely true that Newton did not make hypotheses. What he actually did was to wonder about the causal relationships among the events he observed. His hypotheses were created on the spot, as it were, without the general rigorous formulation of the hypothetico-deductive method. I think all investigators make these on-the-spot hypotheses. Some call them hunches; I choose to call them *hypothesitos* which is semi-Spanish for "little hypotheses."

Another key principle of the informal theoretical group is the almost exclusive reliance on careful investigation of the single case rather than a large group of subjects. It has been traditional in the last century to collect large numbers of subjects

---

* An interesting and amusing illustration of the step-by-step development of an experiment may be found in Skinner's "Case History in Scientific Method" which appeared in 1956 (85).

in order to obtain what is generally referred to as a representative sample, or a sufficiently large group from which to make general hypotheses. In using such a group approach, it is necessary to remember that the individual tends to become somewhat obscured. All the individuals are lumped together in a statistical entity that has no real existence. For example, you may speak of the interest pattern of the adolescent as though there were *an* adolescent representative of all members of such a group (reminiscent of the Platonic "idea" of a class, such as a chair that represents the concept of a chair). All you are doing is pooling the most frequently encountered interests (such as sports, perhaps) of a particular group and noting that the average adolescent has this cluster of interests. It tells you little or nothing of a particular adolescent who lives across the street from you, except what you might possibly expect to find. Only an investigation of the individual can tell you whether or not his interest pattern conforms or deviates from the average. Then, if you wish to relate his performance to the group from which he is drawn, you may place him as having less than average adolescent interests, meaning that he deviates from the norm to some degree.

Perhaps a more specific illustration may be drawn from the height distribution of a group. For example, a high school senior class has an average height of 5'8", meaning that roughly two-thirds of the class cluster around that mean. This does not make a boy of 5' any taller nor a boy of 6' any shorter. It might be important to know the average height for such purposes as planning a procession; if, however, you wanted to order caps and gowns for the class it would obviously be necessary to take each individual's measurement.

In considering the importance of concentrating on the individual, Sidman, in a discussion of Skinner, comments (84):

Skinner's rejection of "confidence level statistics" derives from his clearly stated interest in the behavior of the individual. This interest dictates an experimental design different from that generally used in psychology. Instead of running groups of animals and averaging their data, it becomes necessary to run individual animals through all of the experimental manipulations. Each animal thus constitutes a replication of the experiment, which not only affords an opportunity for detecting differences among animals, but also actually imposes the obligation to report them and, where possible, to *explain* them. The procedure of treating differences among animals as lawful, rather than as examples of the capriciousness of nature or of the experimental techniques, provides Skinner with one of his substitutes for statistical treatment. Experimentation is continued until the variables responsible for deviant behavior are identified. A corollary of this point of view is that any behavioral effect repeatedly demonstrated in the same animal is a lawful phenomenon.

Sidman believes that the control of data in research does not depend on the amassing of large groups of subjects or even large samples from an individual subject. He states (78) that "We must consider our science immeasurably enriched each time someone brings another sample of behavior under precise experimental control." He believes that the adequacy of a technique in experimental psychology should be evaluated in terms of the reliability and precision of the control it achieves. This does not necessarily mean that apparatus (as an extension of human operations) is the answer. Apparatus only performs what the human sets up. A human experimenter can count the number of times a pigeon pecks at a key, but his accuracy is dubious in view of the rapidity with which a pigeon can peck— up to fifteen times a second. It is more accurate and simpler to attach a switch to the key so that each time the pigeon pecks, he closes a circuit and puts a pulse into a counter that records the rapid pecking. Obviously this can be extended to ink-writer recorders, timers, and other pieces of equipment for various purposes.

The critical question is the type of data desired and the preci-

sion of control achieved. Sidman offers (79) a good illustration
of this in an account of a drug study:

> There is wide interest in the relations between behavior and
> the action of pharmacologic agents. One important aspect of
> a drug is its time course of action. To illustrate, let us estab-
> lish a baseline of avoidance behavior with the white rat as
> subject. The animal is given a brief shock every 20 seconds
> if it does not press a lever. Each time it presses the lever it
> postpones the next shock for 20 seconds. Under these cir-
> cumstances the rat will learn to press the lever, and will do
> so at a rate sufficiently high to avoid most of the shocks.
> After some experience, the animal will settle down to a
> steady rate of lever pressing which remains constant for
> periods of six hours or longer. Once the avoidance behavior
> has reached this stable state we can then administer a drug,
> e.g., amphetamine sulfate (commonly known as Benzedrine),
> to the animal. Our record of the subject's rate of lever press-
> ing will then display a sequence of departures from its usual
> appearance. A short while after the drug has been adminis-
> tered, the rat will begin to press the lever more and more
> rapidly, and the record will show a smooth acceleration from
> its baseline rate. The rate will reach some limiting value, say
> three to four times higher than usual, and will remain at this
> level for two to three hours. Then it will begin to decline, and
> the record will show a smooth return to its baseline level.
> But the animal will not simply return to its former rate of
> lever pressing. The rate will actually decline below its base-
> line level, and it will remain depressed for several hours.
>
> In order to follow temporal relations between a drug and
> behavior, it is necessary to maintain the behavior at stable
> level over long periods of time. In addition, the measures
> employed to characterize the behavior must be potentially
> variable in either direction. That is to say, the measure, in
> addition to being stable in time, must also be able to increase
> or decrease over a wide range in order to provide a sensitive

test of the drug action. A behavioral control technique that possesses these properties will permit the moment-to-moment recording of the temporal course of the drug action.

In addition, it would be possible in the above study to take physiological recordings, such as blood pressure or muscle readings, concurrently with the behavior recordings so that there could be a clear correlation established between changes in behavior and physiological functioning over a controlled period of time under definitely specified conditions.

Control of the data is essential in any methodology, formal theoretical or informal theoretical, and steps must be taken to insure such control. I have referred to some of them in this chapter. In the next chapter I am going to take up the crucial problem of definition. There is a need to specify the variables with which the experimenter is working. Definition of terms is a basic means of control.

Chapter Four
The Problem of Definition

We have seen in our earlier discussions that measurement is basic to the scientific method and that measurement itself is of two fundamental types. First, the nominal type that asks the question "does the phenomenon exist?" and second, the type of measurement that asks the question "if the phenomenon exists, to what extent does it exist; what is its magnitude or intensity?" In order to be able to formulate some sort of measurement for a phenomenon, one must define it clearly and unequivocally. This brings us to one of the basic problems of the scientific method: the definition of the variables, phenomena, or events with which the scientist is concerned.

On the surface, this might seem like a relatively simple problem. Our daily life is so filled with naming and defining objects. But it is in just this deceptive simplicity that the real problem of definition lies. We're so accustomed to dictionary definitions that we tend to think of these as being clear, unequivocal, and real. At this point I would observe that a major error in scientific method is the uncritical transfer of dictionary definitions to scientific method, for dictionary definitions do not define in a scientific manner. Skinner (92) has noted that:

> Theories of meaning usually deal with corresponding arrays of words and things. How do the linguistic entities on one side correspond with the things or events which are their meanings on the other side, and what is the nature of the relation between them called "reference"? Dictionaries seem,

at first blush, to support the notion of such arrays. But dictionaries do not give meanings; at best they give words having the same meanings.

Ultimately there must be some clear operation to which these words may be related.

Ideally, the referent (or referents) should be physical, and agreed upon by observers in defining the object. The optimal description is triangular: the tangible object, the observer, and the defining word.

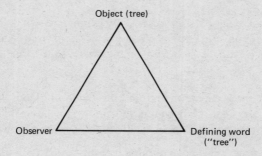

It is not until we get into more abstract kinds of defining words that we get into operational problems. Moving from a "tree" to "knowledge" and "truth" is not only a large philosophical jump but a tremendous semantic leap as well.

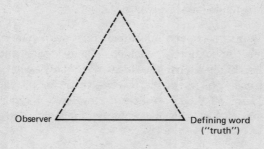

Many years ago Stuart Chase, in a book entitled *The Tyranny of Words,* suggested a useful technique. He asked that "abstract words and phrases without discoverable referents would register a semantic blank, noises without meaning." As an example (36), he drew upon a political speech by an aspiring Hitler:

> The Aryan Fatherland, which has nursed the souls of heroes, calls upon you for the supreme sacrifice which you, in whom flows heroic blood, will not fail, and which will echo forever down the corridors of history.

What Chase suggests is that every time you come across a word that does not have a clear physical referent, you simply substitute "blab." Thus he translates (37) the Hitlerian speech as:

> The blab blab, which has nursed the blabs of blabs, calls upon you for the blab blab which you, in whom flows blab blood, will not fail, and which will echo blab down the blabs of blab.

This is a technique that might well be applied to most commencement addresses, political speeches, and much professorial comment. With regard to the latter, Chase (38) also gives an illustrative example:

> Education implies teaching. Teaching implies knowledge. Knowledge is truth. The truth is everywhere the same. Hence education should be everywhere the same.

Here the writer, a famous educator, starts with four high-order abstractions: "education," "teaching," "knowledge," and "truth." He then establishes absolute identity: "knowledge is truth." Then, as Chase observes, there's one truth for all places, and presumably for all times. While we may have a vague general idea of what this means, it would be impossible, in practical terms, to plan a curriculum for a real school with real children on the basis of something that we must take for granted as having abstract and, indeed comforting, intellectual sound.

Three Levels of Definition

To pursue the problem of definition a bit further, let me suggest that there are three levels of definition, which I call *daily, poetic,* and *scientific.* The daily definition is one that is universally accepted and for which there is a general understanding. The poetic definition need not be universally accepted nor generally understood, but is treated as belonging within the realm of individual license and creativity. The scientific definition is restricted to a limited group for which the definition must have specific meaning. To take an example, suppose we define the moon from the standpoint of daily, poetic, and scientific com-munication. The daily definition of the moon might be "a round, heavenly body that revolves around the earth, which reflects the sun's light and becomes full once a month." The poetic definition might be something along the lines of "a silver crescent, glowingly set against the velvet blackness of the brooding sky." Finally, a scientific definition might be some-thing like "a heavenly body, a satellite of the planet earth (the third planet in the system of Sol) that revolves around the planet once every twenty-eight days, has a mean distance from the earth of approximately 238,000 miles and a diameter of approximately 2,160 miles, and reflects the light of the sun (Sol)."

It might be noted that an accurate definition of the moon from a scientific standpoint must inevitably define such things as planet and the system of Sol (which is a Type GO star), and so on. The three types of definition obviously differ in their clarity and their specificity. As I mentioned, a major error is the transference of a daily definition (or, less likely, a poetic one) to scientific usage. An astronomer could hardly do meaningful scientific measurements using concepts that would be acceptable in daily conversation, such as "becoming full once a month." The scientific definition must deal with specific and unequivocal description. It might also be observed at this point that the transfer of scientific communication to the daily or poetic realm would be equally inappropriate. The lover at a lakeside who describes the moon to his sweetheart as the satellite of the third planet, Earth, in the system of Sol, would probably be as unsuccessful as a poetic astronomer at a scientific meeting. In daily conversation such descriptions are considered pedantic.

The Problem of Clarity

It cannot be overemphasized that a major error in scientific method is the use of daily definitions. Yet this is a very frequent problem in certain types of research, especially that dealing with human behavior and clinical problems. For example, take the word "anxiety," a common word for which there is a fairly clear daily definition. Even a word like personality, which has a large number of meanings,* is relatively clearly understood in certain contexts, even though these usages differ. For example, personality is something that one can have ("he has a lot of personality"). The fact that you can talk about "a lot of" suggests that there is some rough scale of magnitude going from

---

* Probably too many meanings, or "surplus meanings," in Hans Reichenbach's sense (72). Marx (66) has commented on this in observing that concepts with surplus meanings may be "tolerated in the early prescientific development of a field but their replacement by constructs more closely and necessarily tied to the data must occur for scientific advance." This is the major point with which we deal in this chapter.

little to lot. It is something that can be treated with a value judgment ("I don't like his personality"). It designates certain identifying characteristics, such as "he is a Hollywood personality." These are all daily definitions that have relative clarity within the specific usages for which they are designed. Like the word anxiety, the word personality leads to confusion when scientific research is attempted. To talk about a "personality disorder" suggests that something is disturbed, but what? Only by rendering a vague daily term such as "personality" meaningful and subject to scientific definition can any significant research be attempted.

Certainly textbooks are not the final arbiters of definition, as may be seen in the following definition of anxiety from a standard textbook in psychiatry (45): "Anxiety, in a sense, is the ego's warning mechanism that something is awry within the personality. The ego itself uses anxiety to indicate that either something within the id or something in the super-ego threatens the ego." While there may be some general understanding of such a statement, it is apparent that scientific understanding could never emerge from it. In order to make such a definition meaningful, ego, superego, personality, id, and anxiety itself must be defined in clear and unequivocal terms, ultimately to be related to observed demonstrable and repeatable events tied to the data.

There is also a touch of circularity in any such case in which the entity to be defined becomes part of the definition. Skinner, as we have noted, has indicated that dictionaries do not give true definitions or meanings of a word, but generally give other words that have the same meaning. In an involuted definition there is a loss of clarity—so in addition to the book definition of "anxiety," we find definitions of depression, such as "heightened sadness" or "feelings of despair," which simply tell us that depression is depression.

Related to this problem is Bertrand Russell's theory of types, which says that an entity cannot be used to define itself. To illustrate this he has proposed a square as follows:

```
┌─────────────────────────┐
│                         │
│   Every statement       │
│   in this square        │
│   is false.             │
│                         │
└─────────────────────────┘
```

If the statement is true, then it is obviously false. If the statement is false, it is patently true. The proposition that a statement whose terms are properly defined cannot logically be both true and false is known in epistomology as the Law of the Excluded Middle.

I mentioned earlier that a definition of the moon might ultimately require further definitions of planets and satellites and other terms used in a scientific definition. But this kind of definition is different from that required for terms such as "id" and "ego" and "personality." The former kind (defining the moon) may be related to observable and demonstrable events, while personality, id, and ego always remain formal verbal symbols. I'll touch upon this also as we continue our discussion.

One phase of this problem of definition may be summed up by quoting from Willard Quine (69) who observed that "the less a science has advanced the more its terminology tends to rest upon an uncritical assumption of mutual understanding." When individuals communicate observations with mutually understood but vague terms (such as "personality"), instead of with terms based on scientific grounds, research is retarded. To bring up another example, if one were to go through research dealing with psychotherapy (loosely defined as the treatment of emotional problems), one would come upon the term "improvement" used widely to indicate a change in the person's behavior. Yet rarely is there any clear definition of what is meant by improvement. If you were to ask a psychotherapist what he meant by improvement, he might say "Well, everyone knows what improvement means," just as he might say "everyone knows what anxiety means" or "everyone knows what personality means." This is the use of the mutually understood, universally accepted, daily definition in a situation that demands scientific definition. To say that "everyone knows . . ." is to beg the question and avoid the major issue of clarity and certainty of definition. The mutual assumption of understanding, as Quine has suggested, is indeed an immature approach to scientific method.

An Attempt at Clarity and Certainty: The Operational Definition

What have we to offer in the way of a meaningful scientific definition? Fundamental to all scientific method is the operational definition. While there are problems with regard to the operational definition, by and large it is clear that scientific method depends upon it. It is defined by Rapoport (71) in the following terms: "An operational definition tells *what to do* to experience the thing defined. Asked to define the coefficient of friction, a physicist says something like this: 'If a block of some material is dragged horizontally over a surface, the force necessary to drag it will, within limits, be proportional to the weight of the block. Thus the ratio of the dragging force to the weight is a constant quantity. This quantity is the coefficient of friction between the two surfaces.' The physicist defines the terms by telling *how to proceed* and *what to observe*." The operational definition of a dish, it has been suggested, is its recipe.

In scientific method, we need to have items that allow for operational definition, although it is undoubtedly true that the very nature of the language itself may preclude complete operationalism. The important thing is to emphasize the necessity for approaching this goal by eliminating the mutually understood but vague terms (in Quine's sense) that impede adequate communication. The fact that this is a problem in psychiatric communication may be illustrated in the following quotation from the *Diagnostic and Statistical Manual: Mental Disorders*, published by the American Psychiatric Association (44), in which the chronic brain syndrome is described: "The chronic organic brain syndromes result from relatively permanent, more or less irreversible diffuse impairment of cerebral tissue function."

I would say that in order for this definition to approach genuine utility as a verbal statement and to have operational meaning, the qualifying aspects of "*relatively* permanent" and "*more or less* irreversible" would have to be made more operationally sound.

Recall where the term "nomenclature" came from originally. It started with the *nomen clator,* a servant employed by a Roman gentleman to walk in front of him and to call out the names of approaching individuals. This service was very helpful, inasmuch as it freed the gentleman from having to remember the names of all the citizenry whom he approached. The *nomen clator* would call out the name "Publius Ovidius Naso," enabling the gentleman to greet him properly. If the *nomen clator* had said, "It's *probably* Publius Ovidius Naso" or "I'm *pretty* sure it's Publius Ovidius Naso," his nomenclature, and probably his position, would have been in considerable jeopardy.

It is apparent that the operational definition starts with observation. The observer records and reports facts and tries to communicate these in a manner that will give maximal clarity. One of the objections to maximal clarity is that the number of definitions involved may become exceptionally cumbersome. The closer one approaches certainty and clarity, the more specific and particular one becomes, while science itself must ultimately lead to generality and prediction. I don't believe that this is a legitimate objection to the use of operational definition. I think that the number of definitions required depends upon the specific circumstance. Percy Bridgman (24) has suggested that common usage prefers ambiguity and a small number of words to clarity and a great number of words.

But this is not entirely true. For example, in our own particular culture there is one word for snow and while we may give qualifying characteristics to this, such as hard, soft, crusty or slushy, common usage does indeed prefer ambiguity to a large number of words describing snow. In the Eskimo culture, however, in which one's life and livelihood depend upon a precise knowledge of the type of snow, there are reported to be thirty words to describe different kinds of snow, each one having a different form. Clyde Kluckhohn (59) has observed that different cultures may emphasize different areas, just as the Eskimo emphasizes the discriminating descriptions of snow. He notes that English "is very discriminating about flocking behavior: we speak of schools of fish, herds of cattle, flocks of sheep, coveys of quail, prides of lions, etc." We can only assume that a culture that develops discrimination about flocking has a need for such discriminations, while other cultures appear satisfied with indicating only that there are "many" sheep or cattle, although I confess I cannot comprehend the need for such fine differentiations. It might even be considered a pack of nonsense!

A single word may be used in many different contexts provided there is clear operational specificity for each use. For example, the word "key" has over twenty meanings in English, each one related to a specific operational referent (music, fraternity, house, and so on). Perhaps this could also be done with greater operational clarity for the many-sided word "personality."

It has been done, in a rudimentary sort of factor analysis, by a group of psychologists (100) who tried to find some consistent meaning in the word "emotion," for which they found over twenty definitions. When these psychologists factored out the element common to all the definitions of emotions, they found one characteristic appearing in all: altered activity of the autonomic nervous system. It is obvious that a layman's definition of emotion wouldn't be apt to bring in that particular phrase, but his description of the behavior involved would probably indicate an increase in heart rate or perspiration, or something similar in physiological activity. These are altered activities of the autonomic nervous system and go along with descriptions couched in more professional terms. When a factor can be pinpointed, this gives us the beginning of a more satisfactory definition of a word such as emotion. We have something that is measurable. (And you know how fond I am of things that are measurable.)

The context of—or stimuli that evoked—the altered physiological state is crucial to defining the emotion. For example, suppose you are sitting in class when the door bursts open and a young man runs in. His face is red and slightly perspiring, he is breathing rapidly and somewhat erratically, his movements are quick and excited. He could be in a rage, very scared, or perhaps sexually aroused by the girl who was climbing the stairs before him. To define the emotional state is to determine the situation that aroused it—exercising a certain amount of caution, of course.

Observations always must start with specific, clear, and restricted definition. Only on this basis can there be any movement toward a correlation of specific observations, making for a more general body of knowledge.

A frequent objection to operational definitions is that they ultimately push the definer into a corner. Rapoport (70) has commented on this with an amusing illustration in which he points out that a strict logical positivist, using his principles and standing by them completely, could not say " 'There is a black sheep.' He could only say, 'I see a sheep, one side of which is black.' If asked whether he did not really believe it was a black sheep, he might say, 'My previous experiences with sheep whose one side was black lead me to expect that if the sheep turned around, I should receive similar sense data.' " This description may appear ludicrous since the observer sounds overly compulsive in his description. But if one were to substitute the word moon for sheep, it becomes a different matter.

Until recently, an observer could only say "there is the moon, one side of which has craters," because no one had seen the other side of the moon and experience limited us to conjecture about the other side. In other words, we have seen many sides of sheep and have the experience that allows us to infer (with a high degree of probability) that a sheep will be the same color on both sides. While there was certainly a good degree of probability that the other side of the moon would have craters, there was no experience that allowed us to make such an inference. The operational definition or logical positivist description of the moon had to be restricted to a description of what was currently observed.

Another objection to operational definition that has occasionally been raised is that it is possible to give operational definition to symbolic entities and therefore the definition is robbed of operational clarity. This is not really a significant problem, inasmuch as science always deals with two types of propositions, which have been described as formal and empirical. S. Stevens (93), for example, in discussing the operational method has observed that "hypotheses . . . can be only formal statements—operationally empty—until they are demonstrated." In clarifying this, he makes a distinction between formal and empirical propositions, saying that formal propositions are symbolic and have no empirical reference; "they are language, mathematics, and logic *as such.*" For example, it is possible to state in a formal proposition that $X = a + b^2$ without any reference to the objects or events described by X, a, or b.

Empirical propositions, on the other hand, "are those in which these arrays of symbols have been identified with observable events." Rapoport (71) has described this also in terms of a propositional function, noting that the propositional function allows a hypothetical statement to be made, such as *X is green.* It is impossible to tell from this formal statement whether it is true or false. If X is grass, there is demonstrable truth; if X is milk, it may be considered false. Mathematical symbols, as a whole, need no immediate empirical reference but may exist within a purely formal structure.

Formal symbols may appear in operational definitions, as in the following example. A psychologist is describing the conditions under which he performed a certain experiment and notes in defining "hunger" (a subjective daily definition that he attempts to render operational): "The rats in this experiment were deprived of food for a period of 72 hours," an accepted procedure for rendering an animal hungry. The word "hour" is a formal symbolic word that has a relationship to, but is removed from, a pure physical event. We have discussed this earlier (page 57) in considering levels of measurement, but a brief recapitulation of the principle in this different area may be of some help. The psychologist uses the term "hour," a nonphysical, verbal, formal symbol which has come to be the sign designating a specific passage of time indicated by the movement of a pair of hands around the face of a clock. The movement of the hands is a physical operation which has been given symbolic designation (second, minute, hour). The final physical operation is the movement inside the clock itself that produced the movement of the hands. A clock is a physical model of the apparent rhythmic motion of the sun. Thus, when a psychologist says he has deprived a rat of food for 72 hours (thereby defining hunger), he is using a verbal symbolic definition related to two other levels of definition of movement—both physical—signifying passage of time and the clock model. He need not go into this when making his statement, because it is known.

The critical point made by this illustration is that verbal, symbolic definitions or terms may be used provided there are some data to which they can be related and provided these data are physical operations. Defining anxiety, in the example given earlier, in terms of egos, ids, and personality merely compounds the problem because there is never any physical operation to which these purely formal, verbal symbols can be related.

Inferred and Invented Concepts

Decidedly related to the above is the question of *inferred* and *invented* concepts. It is obvious that many of the concepts with which the scientist works are inferred from data and that others are constructed to account for certain observed events. For example, the atom is an inferred concept which has its origin in observed data and which presumably exists in a real sense. The discovery or observation of the atom itself will depend upon the development of finer and finer measurements. And so, while the term atom may have formal properties and be differentially related to physical events, ultimately it may itself be a physically observed event. The term hypothetical construct has been used to describe this type of inferred concept presumed to exist and for which it is expected that experience will provide later disclosure.

In contrast to the hypothetical construct or inferred concept, there is the invented concept (referred to frequently as an intervening variable) used by the experimenter to account for events that he has observed. Heredity and learning are such intervening variables. Neither heredity nor learning may be seen in a physical sense, but they are nonetheless operationally defined as invented concepts. To illustrate this further, heredity is an intervening variable which has been invented to account for certain observed physical events. At one point in history, the gene and chromosome were hypothetical constructs which were inferred as mechanisms of the transmission of heredity. Genes and chromosomes have physical reality and as such can be disclosed. Heredity is not a physical event but a concept created to account for physical operations. Similarly, learning is an intervening variable; but a change in the neurophysiological structure of the brain, which may be inferred to occur in learning, has not been clearly isolated and remains an hypothetical construct. It is rooted in data and is presumed to exist as a physical operation. Further research may yield more information.

To sum up this aspect of the discussion of operational methods, I would like to turn to Herbert Feigl (46), who has set up the following criteria for operational methods, which I have modified:

1. They should be logically consistent, that is, derived logically one from the other and be related to other operational definitions.
2. They should be definite, preferably quantitative.
3. They should be empirically based, linked to the observable.
4. They should be technically possible, subject to experimental manipulation.
5. They should be intersubjective and repeatable, demonstrable in different species and repeatable by different experimenters.
6. They should aim at the creation of concepts that will allow for laws or theories of greater predictiveness.

It is obvious from the above that Feigl's concept of operational methodology is clearly related to our previous discussion of theory and its construction dealing with logically derived, consistent terminology for data that are measurable, based on observation, subject to manipulation for testing, repeatable from subject to subject and experimenter to experimenter and, finally, aimed at the creation of some order or cohesion of facts into a system.

One often hears the cliché that nature has all the answers available and it is up to the experimenter to find the right question to pose. There is a great deal of truth in this, and I would suggest that it is only through the use of clarity in operational definition of one's variables that the right questions may be posed.

Chapter Five
The Laboratory and the "Real World": Animal and Human Research

Many people seem to believe that results found in the laboratory, often with lower organisms such as white rats, are not really applicable to practical problems of the human, everyday world. Egon Brunswik's concept of the "representative design" may be considered here. Briefly, a representative design characterizes an experiment that has a minimum of artificiality and a maximum of control. It is an ideal design in that it brings the problems of the "real world" together with the exact methods of the experimental laboratory. As may be seen in the following figure, an ideal experiment is one at the point where reality and control cross, but as so often happens with ideals, most

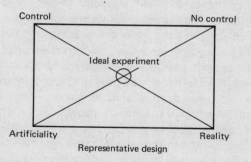

Representative design

experiments fall short of perfection. This does not mean that the ideal criterion should be overlooked. Some compromise is always experienced in applying laboratory methods to larger problems but this is, as we have seen (page 49), part of the methodology of science by which the experimenter, through controlled procedures, attempts to establish the probability that a particular explanation is correct. Ideally, if one wished to find out what a particular city's population said about a candidate at election time, one would interview every citizen. The compromise with such an ideal is rendered necessary by the impossibility of such a task; the time alone required to interview, say, a million people, would be prohibitive. So the pollster takes a *representative sample,* hoping to slice out a segment of the population that represents a cross section of the whole, with enough workers, businessmen, professional people, etcetera, to form a microcosm of the city. Whether or not he has been successful in his representative sample is always a problem for poll-takers, but it is, nonetheless, illustrative of a laboratory procedure used in a real situation to establish probabilities of an event's occurrence; that is, the probability of one candidate emerging victorious over the other. Based on his poll, he bets that his guess is correct by stating the possible voting percentages, perhaps 55 percent for Candidate A, 40 percent for Candidate B, 5 percent Undecided. The many factors that might play a part in shifting such odds are taken into consideration up to the last moment of the election. To be sure, poll taking represents an adaptation of the laboratory procedure of sampling but lacks the precision of the laboratory with regard to precise control of the variables after the selection of the subject population, although, here, once again, is an excellent illustration of the way improved instrumentation results in improved data collection and analysis. The use of the high-speed computer, with its capability for storing enormous numbers of facts—population characteristics, previous voting records, and similar data in a community—coupled with its ability to integrate rapidly and analyze stored and new information, has enabled pollsters to develop infinitely greater degrees of accuracy in prediction.

A criticism often leveled at the laboratory is that it deals with trivial facts. As we have seen (page 52), the narrower a focus of activity is, the easier it is to measure, and so the objection is heard that laboratory results are not solutions to problems, but only abstracted and unimportant facts. In psychology, for example, one might ask: of what relevance to the protean problems of human behavior is it if a rat turns left in a maze or if a pigeon learns to discriminate between a circle and a square? Beyond any possible relevance to problems in human learning, there is still another consideration: science progresses by accumulating unities among seemingly diverse and disparate facts. Thus it is by the discovery of what may appear to be superficially unimportant details that science builds its superstructure of theory. Perhaps most important of all, one discovery leads to another as one result points out another problem. Science is a regenerative discipline where one fact leads to other possible events in an ever-widening vortex of new information. As Bronowski (28) has stated it:

> I do not think that truth becomes more primitive if we pursue it to simpler facts. For no fact in the world is instant, infinitesimal and ultimate, a single mark. There are, I hold, no atomic facts; in the language of science every fact is a field.

But Why Animals?

There still remains the question, But why animals? Assuming that a person goes into psychology as a career or signs up for a psychology course out of interest in human behavior, why does he get sidetracked into working with the ubiquitous white rat? And what does this have to do with human behavior? Skinner (91) has discussed this question:

> We study the behavior of animals because it is simpler. Basic processes are revealed more easily and can be recorded over longer periods of time. Our observations are not complicated by the social relation between subject and experimenter. Conditions may be better controlled. We may

arrange genetic histories to control certain variables and special life histories to control others—for example, if we are interested in how an organism learns to see, we can raise an animal in darkness until the experiment is begun. We are also able to control current circumstances to an extent not easily realized in human behavior—for example, we can vary states of deprivation over wide ranges. These are advantages which should not be dismissed on the *a priori* contention that human behavior is inevitably set apart as a separate field. . . . It would be rash to assert at this point that there is no essential difference between human behavior and the behavior of lower species; but until an attempt has been made to deal with both in the same terms, it would be equally rash to assert that there is.

In the above quotation, Skinner illustrates some aspects of the use of animals in research, particularly the possibilities of doing certain kinds of experiments with animals that could not be conveniently performed on humans, yielding facts that can become increasingly relevant and important to human behavior. He also states a critical point germane to the question of the differences between animal and human behavior: we cannot be rash enough to assert similarities or differences until we have the data.

One reason, then, for animal research is the *feasibility* of conducting research with animals that could not be carried out on human subjects. Brain functioning, for example, is not as clearcut an area as some texts portray it to be in the interests of simplicity. Volumes have been written on such everyday events as sleep and consciousness without giving a truly clear definition of these events. Much of the work accomplished in the important study of brain functioning has been done on animals, in which areas of the brain have been removed, stimulated with electrical current, or subjected to chemical and surgical injury, all with an eye toward seeking out the answers to the structure and function of the brain and central nervous system. Could these experiments have been performed on humans? Obviously not. No systematic surgical ablation of or implantation of electrodes into the brain of a human subject to study such questions as the effect of electrical stimulation of brain centers would be possible. Yet for the solution of such crucial questions as causes of epilepsy and other neurological diseases, such as multiple sclerosis, such experiments—possible only on animals—must be performed.

The question of which animal to use in experimental work is another matter. Some experiments tend to dictate the species used. For example, rats lack color vision, and an experiment requiring color discrimination could not use rats as subjects. Pigeons, on the other hand, have excellent vision, including color vision, and might be good subjects for such an experiment. Their exceptionally high rate of response in pecking at a key in an experimental box also has obvious advantages in an experiment requiring high rates of response. Monkeys and chimpanzees also have good response rates and their advantages in size and similarity to humans in many respects make them important experimental animals. If one wished to use an animal whose behavior most closely resembled human behavior (partly by species characteristic and partly by close human contact), in all probability he would select the dog (Does the name Pavlov ring a bell?). And the independence of the cat is not confined to the home and hearth. Cats are notoriously recalcitrant experimental subjects in behavioral research.

Genetic studies of species with short life spans, allowing for many generations of study, can be done only with animals such as the fruitfly. It would be impossible for an experimenter to go through more than two or three generations of humans himself in a genetic study and it would also be impossible to manipulate genetic factors for study. This can be done with animals.

There are other reasons to choose particular animals as experimental subjects. L. K. Bustad suggests that the busy experimenter who has to leave town every once in a while to consult in Washington might wish to use the big brown bat. As Bustad (33) notes:

> It weighs only 25 grams, doesn't eat much, and has minimal housing requirements. The big advantage is that, should one find that an absence of a month or two is suddenly necessary, this experimental subject may be placed in a cigar box with a supply of water and stored in a refrigerator. Upon returning from travel status, the investigator may retrieve his bat from the refrigerator and initiate his experiment after less than an hour's thawing time. This animal has been utilized in studies of micro-circulation and of the thyroid gland.

He also suggests that the armadillo might be a good experimental animal. He has me interested, as a researcher in underwater behavior and physiology, because the armadillo can hold his breath for ten minutes and incur a huge oxygen debt. Among the other advantages that Bustad notes is that the armadillo is hearty, "he does not bite or kick," and will eat anything. The real advantage for a research worker is that "the female gives birth to monozygotic quadruplets." Thus the experimenter may remove one fetus of a quadruplet litter "at different stages of development without affecting the other fetuses . . . ." This possibility has an exciting research potential, for studies have shown that different litters of armadillos have shown differing characteristics. With a single uterine environment held under strict control, other relevant genetic and environmental variables may be studied most carefully.

Obviously, the animal chosen for a particular experiment, like the experimental methodology and the equipment, must be appropriate to the purpose of the experiment.

It is true that, with all the intellectual reasons for using certain experimental animals, a researcher may develop preferences for one species over another and find many of his experiments dictated by his favorite animal. I confess to being a pigeon man, and many of my experiments are conducted with these birds as subjects. Some experiments—with drugs, for example—may be better done with rats or primates, and they become the subjects. And another area of investigation in which I am engaged is the study of speech, a project necessarily requiring human subjects.

The student interested in research should avail himself of every chance to work with different species in different kinds of experiments and let his own reinforcement history (in terms of what he finds most rewarding) lead him.

To return to Skinner's statement that it is too early to assert differences or similarities between animal and human behavior, let us now consider an important aspect of this question. Critics of extrapolations from animal to human behavior see a gap that cannot be bridged between the behavior of animals and human beings. However, those of us who see the relevance of some animal work to human behavior often suggest that there are more universals than may appear obvious. One example is found in programmed learning and teaching machines used with human students, the basis for which is to be found in previous learning research using pigeons as subjects. With the need for more experimentation in basic laws of learning, the problem may be at best academic, but one fact stands out clearly and deserves attention: there is an erroneous approach to analogy between human and animal behavior that only leads to further confusion. This analogue approach is based on the assumption that to study a phenomenon in animals that is related to human behavior it is necessary to set up a completely analogous condition—for example, that to study psychotic behavior, we must render a rat psychotic. Let us consider the analogue error in greater detail because of its centrality to the problem.

The Analogue Error

When a psychologist does work with animal subjects in an experiment, someone may say, "This is all very interesting but what does it have to do with human behavior? It's nice that you have been able to produce ulcers in white rats, but what does that tell us about ulcers in people?" This is the heart of the analogue error: the assumption that there must be a one-to-one relationship between the two events. If we wish to study disordered behavior in animals it is erroneously assumed that we must reproduce the same type of behavior disorder found in humans. But, as Sidman (80) observes, ". . . why should we expect a rat's psychosis to bear any surface resemblance to that of a human being?" He goes on to suggest that a certain class of factors may result in a human's going to live in a cave (in what the culture would consider a psychotic manner), while the same class of factors in a rat may lead him to continue to press a bar to get fed long after the food magazine has been withdrawn. Our problem is not to create an analogue of human psychotic behavior in the rat but rather, as Sidman further notes (81), to obtain "sufficient understanding of both rats and men to be able to recognize resemblances in behavioral processes. We must be able to classify our variables in such a manner that we can recognize similarities in their principles of operation, in spite of the fact that their physical specifications may be quite different."

Let me present a more detailed example of such an approach by taking a common human behavioral problem—depression. If you were to describe a person who is depressed, you might say, among other things, that he is listless, has lost his appetite, doesn't do much, looks sad, lies around the house or sits and stares at his feet, and talks in a low and monotonous voice (if he talks at all). All of these are behavioral descriptions which might fall under a general class of lowered activity and unresponsiveness. Suppose we were able to determine that an event was associated with this generalized unresponsiveness, for instance, the loss of his fiancée. The observer reports that the person received a letter from his girl, breaking their engagement, and began to exhibit behavior similar to that described above. He wouldn't eat, paid little attention to his friends, missed classes, spent much of his time lying in bed staring at the ceiling, and generally looked sad. We can say, in technical terminology, that a generalized reinforcer was withdrawn and appeared to be the occasion for the lowered responsiveness or, as the others in the dormitory said, "His girl broke off with him and he's depressed."

It is manifestly impossible to reproduce those exact conditions in the laboratory; that is, to have a monkey receive a Dear John letter. But we can set up a study in which behavioral processes may be investigated which might have some relationship. Let us start with a model of the student's behavior: S will stand for stimulus and P for person, the student. The schema might be sketched as follows:

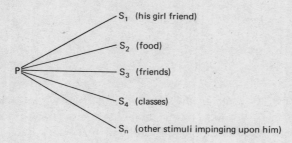

S_1 (his girl friend)

S_2 (food)

P S_3 (friends)

S_4 (classes)

S_n (other stimuli impinging upon him)

S_1, his fiancée, has been removed, breaking the responsiveness to that particular type of stimulation. The effect of extinction (withdrawing the positive reinforcement or pleasurable consequences of the relationship) spreads to the other stimuli so that he becomes unresponsive to S_2, S_3, S_4, and S_n. The spread of effect of conditioning and extinction is well known in learning research. So now we have the beginning of a model. We might elaborate on this a bit further and consider other aspects to study. Before the actual break-up of the engagement, it is possible that there were events that signalled a disturbance in the relationship between the student and his girl. Perhaps one day he saw her walking in the park with a man, holding hands. This would probably be a disturbing event, a stimulus that might warn him of impending unpleasant events. His behavior in the face of a warning stimulus such as this might become agitated, upset, or angry. The letter informing him of the termination of their engagement follows upon such warning stimuli and may be considered the final unpleasant event that occasions the depression. So we can add to our model by placing warning stimuli in the system: S_w (for warning stimulus) appears between the student and S_l (the fiancée).

We can now take this model and see what behavioral processes in the lab may be established to study it, creating conditions appropriate to the problem and manipulating these conditions. As I have mentioned, it would be impossible to set up an experiment in which a monkey's fiancée leaves him, but we can set up an experiment in which a monkey is given a strong generalized reinforcer, perhaps even another monkey. The second monkey would be associated with as many pleasurable reinforcing events as possible. As Sidman says in commenting on such a study (82), "Once the desired relationship has been established between the two monkeys, the second monkey could be removed, leaving the first one bereft of the source of many of its reinforcements. We could then observe any subsequent changes in the behavior of the experimental animal. We might even use a warning stimulus to signal the impending withdrawal of the generalized reinforcer and note the behavior of our monkey in the presence of this stimulus."

The warning stimulus, for example, could be a red light that went on before the second monkey was to be taken away. Do we have a depressed monkey in this case? It doesn't matter whether you call it that or not. If we can establish that there are similarities in the behavioral processes which go on in human and animal upon the removal of a strong rewarding stimulus, it doesn't matter what you call this process. The monkey may refuse to eat or it may gorge itself on bananas, the human may refuse food or turn to liquor. What we are interested in is the behavioral processes of both in the presence of similar conditions.

In sum, the crux of the analogue error is the failure to distinguish between *similarity* and *analogy*. If a person begging on the street learns that wearing shabby clothes, affecting (or really having) a physical deformity, and presenting a pitiful mien will get more money, then we may say that his behavior has been shaped to bring him the most reward. If a bear in a zoo learns that standing on his hind legs and presenting a front view with his paws extended and slightly cupped brings him more peanuts from visitors, we may say also that his behavior has been shaped to be the most rewarding. There is similarity —a particular pattern of behavior is successful and is continued. We may say that both the shabbily dressed human and the standing bear are begging, but this may be anthropomorphically questioning the begging.

Chapter Six
Ethical Considerations in Research

Ethics and Morality in Science

Long debates have occurred within scientific and philosophical circles regarding the ethical and moral characteristics of science. Robert Cohen (39) is one scholar who views science as necessarily being ethically neutral and amoral. "We come to realize again that science is morally neutral. It has not automatically been a force for good. . . . Furthermore, the extension of science to the study of society and history is no guarantee of a humane commitment within the scientific community, nor of moral wisdom within scientific knowledge." A scientist cannot allow questions of an ethical or moral nature to intrude upon his experimentation and methodology. If he has a question about the morality of his research, he should perhaps ask it at the beginning (Shall I get into this area of experimentation; let us say, bacteriological warfare?), or after the experimentation is completed (What applications will be made of my research?—a question posed by the Archbishop of York to British scientists about the uses of the inventions they create; see p. 132). The experimentation itself is tactically determined and directed by scientific method, which is concerned with a different kind of ethical and moral problem, that of honesty and integrity. Stated otherwise, science does not concern itself with *values* during the course of research. But values themselves can be subjected to scientific study.

As M. W. Wartofsky (98) suggests, there are three basic questions regarding the relation of science to value:

1. Is value amenable to scientific study, and may the object of such study be taken as either natural or as human, societal fact? Is there a science of value; that is, is there a rational, validated system by which value can be studied?
2. What values are exhibited *in* science and scientific method? Is there an *ethos* or ethics of science?
3. What is the value *of* science? What larger interest does science subserve or subvert?

In our own scientific method, a major reason that neutrality or amorality exists is tactical. The prevailing scientific method in our culture, as we have seen earlier, is keyed to a probability of events. The concept of probability (page 49) determines the structure of the experimental question: What are the chances that this event will occur, given certain experimental manipulations? Confidence-level statistics are geared to assessing such probabilities within a range of confidence statements; the odds are that this event will most certainly occur (a probability of 1.00). But probability, useful as it is in scientific method, also engenders certain philosophical consequences. It leads, for one thing, to a disbelief in absolutes; few things always or never occur (on your multiple-choice examinations don't you tend to avoid choices that say "never" or "always"?). This disbelief strengthens a world view in which relativism is dominant, and this extends to ethical considerations as well.

The relativistic, probabilistic world view exerts a marked influence upon, and comes under the influence of, the culture in which it stands. Max Weber (99) has pointed out that "the belief in the value of scientific truth is the product of certain cultures and is not a product of man's original nature." To be sure, the reliance upon experimental method as a means toward the truth is, as we shall see, more a characteristic of Western societies than of others and is clearly both a shaper and a product of the Puritan ethic (page 133), which believes in a rationalistic world order that can be discovered (and altered). With a world view that sees events as less than absolute, it is possible to visualize change and ways of restructuring events. Cultural anthropology has contributed importantly to such a view. Florence Kluckhohn (60) has described two world views that vary in their acceptance of the inevitability of absolutes—"man subjugated to nature" and "man versus nature (or *over* nature in the sense of rational mastery of it)." With respect toward disease and death, we may contrast the Latin and Anglo cultures, pointing out that the former, manifested by Mexican values (which are undergoing change), has exhibited a fatalistic acceptance of events (what will be, will be) in which death is seen as natural, absolute, and inevitable. The acceptance of inevitability necessarily restricts action that leads to change; hence Latin acceptance of public health measures such as mass inoculation to prevent disease was delayed by a world view that did not favor resistance to change, even change that might result in death. The attitude of the Anglo culture toward death was summed up by the Welsh poet Dylan Thomas in a poem to his dying father:

> Do not go gentle into that good night.
> Rage, rage against the dying of the light.

This is obviously an overstated and oversimplified contrast, but it has had validity, at least in the past.

The scientific order based on the probabilistic, rationalistic view of the world provides its own ethics of science as a cultural phenomenon. Science and ethics become guides to rational action; as in a democratic society rational action involves an orchestration of independence and interdependence of individuals, so it does in science. Cohen (39) observed that "the ethics of science is the democratic state of a cooperative republic" in which citizens decide policy and ideas are tested with what William James once called a "robust sense of reality." The democratic ethic of science also allows for interdependence and respect. When an Einstein supplants a Newton, he does so not as a beachmaster replacing a vanquished sea lion but rather as a participant in the evolutionary process of discovery—that is, the act of supplanting is committed with the respect properly accorded an elder statesman.

Inevitably, the question of value or ethics in science focuses upon the scientist himself, as a scientist and as a citizen. A scientist may condemn himself if he allows value judgments to interfere with the execution of his research; he may also condemn himself if he is not concerned with value judgments as a citizen. Nowhere has this dilemma been more dramatically demonstrated than in the concern shown by nuclear physicists after World War II (see page 132) regarding the use of the nuclear energy they had developed. This group, referred to somewhat pejoratively by critics as "The League of Frightened Men" (a designation the men themselves agreed to), expressed their anxieties about the applications of atomic power. As scientists they had performed optimally; as humans and citizens they wished to perform equally well.

At times this twofold desire creates something of a problem. Our culture tends to exploit the universal expert. A person successful in one field, such as football, need not know any more about automobile batteries than the ordinary citizen, but he often influences ordinary citizens in their purchasing—by endorsing various products. The scientist may not be as aware of social and political events as he is of experimental methodology, but as a citizen he is morally bound to interact as best he can with his culture. Too often the scientist is not adequately prepared for the complexities that exist in the culture. For example, psychologists who sincerely wish to apply some of their knowledge to social problems often find that their knowledge of the community is sparse. The critical question of who really makes the decisions in a community (Is it the Mayor?) can affect the most worthwhile endeavor. A colleague of mine who was interested in juvenile delinquency in a Southwestern city found that the statistics of minor crime were contaminated because police officers merely reprimanded youths of a certain sociocultural status, yet booked those from lower levels of society, thus distorting the data on frequency and source of crime. In such a case, the psychologist interested in delinquency must first determine the accuracy of the community report. I sincerely believe that most of us are ill-equipped by training to make such a determination. The average first-year student of social work probably knows more about community organization than the majority of Ph.D.s in psychology.

The preceding paragraph may seem pessimistic. It is not intended to be. I wish to emphasize that the scientist who seeks to express citizen concern and participate in the application of scientific knowledge to the solution of important community problems must be as rigorous and as well-equipped to take on such applications as he is to conduct his experimentation. Otherwise, he is in danger of creating a large cadre of compassionate incompetents who mean well.

In sum, the ethics of science exists. It exists as a system of rationalistic, industrious pursuit of facts. The choice of an area of research and the applications of the research accomplished are moral concerns for the scientist; the conduct of the research is not, except as it involves honesty and integrity of performance.

Advances in technology and science often place new ethical concerns before the scientist. For example, in recent years the development of artificial kidneys and the means of keeping heart activity going in patients who otherwise would have died, coupled with the advances in organ transplants, have created ethical dilemmas for scientists. Consider the question "How are we now to define death?" Electrical stimulation can keep a heart going, so the traditional definition of death as "heart stoppage" may not be appropriate. This realization has led in recent years to reexamination of death as irreversible cerebral stoppage. The brain then comes to be considered the center of life rather than the heart. Recent statements have clearly focused on neurological signs. For these, Ivan (57) and the Canadian Medical Association (34) suggest unreceptivity and unresponsivity of the patient to externally applied stimuli; no move-ments or breathing that can be detected, either as spontaneous or as evoked by pain, touch, sound, or light; no elicitable reflexes; and finally, the flat electroencephalogram (EEG, or brain wave). Thus the definition of death becomes a matter of irreversible brain damage with the assumption that, given artificial means of stimulating the heart or oxygenating blood through the tis-sues of the body, unless the individual is able to function on his own (through the mechanism of cerebral activity) to pro-vide life support for such vital organs as the heart, he is func-tionally dead. The theological-philosophical questions that such approaches involve are obviously important.

Public Concern with Research

There is no doubt that one of the thorniest problems faced by researchers is that of gaining maximal information about the subjects used in the studies within a humane ethical frame-work. Research procedures have frequently been a source of concern and, indeed, alarm to the nonscientist. The layman's image of the scientist (which will be explored more thoroughly in the following chapter) is usually not an accurate one. The most apparent misconceptions about science and the scientist are those concerning experimental procedures. Occasionally, scientists receive letters from people who have read about some research (usually in the newspapers) and who express strong concern about the procedures used. Often there is insufficient information given in the news story to allow for adequate understanding of the purpose of the research, the techniques, and, in particular, the many humane safeguards taken to prevent unnecessary pain and discomfort to the ani-mals used. An example of such a situation may be drawn from the experience of a colleague of mine who was working with the development of vision, a critical problem of great impor-tance to human welfare and science. A woman read of the experiments, in which kittens were used because of the similarity of their visual development to humans and the feasibility of carrying out intensive studies of change in an animal that matures quickly. This woman, obviously a sincere animal lover, took the time to write a letter to the university in which this research was going on, protesting what she believed to be cruel and unnecessary practices in the laboratory. Her letter follows:

I've learned of experiments on helpless kittens and cats perpetrated in laboratories of your University, financed by taxpayers' money. I feel sure you do not know about them.

Contact lenses were put into the eyes of young, UNANES-THETICIZED kittens, and later the visual nerve cells in their brains were connected to micro-electrodes, to compare them with cats who had had visual experience while growing up.

Many people, some of them famous, have been wearing contact lenses very successfully a long time. SURELY, it was a cruel, USELESS WASTE of money, time and labor?

Doubtless, there are many other cruel experiments going on at your University, a black stain on its fair name. WHAT is the effect on the character of the experimenters?

The newspaper story was written with a high degree of accuracy and there was, of course, human interest value and some humor in a scientist grinding contact lenses for kittens. What was not clearly conveyed in the story was the general purpose of the experiments. The letter written in response to her letter tried to provide the needed background and information:

We sincerely appreciate your concern about the animals used in the research and wish to assure you that under no circumstances do any of the animals suffer any pain whatever. The micro-electrodes you have read about which are used to study nerve cells are not a great deal different from the electroencephalographic studies done on humans in hospitals to detect the presence of brain tumor or epilepsy. The purpose of the contact lenses, which do not even provide discomfort for the kittens, is not to see whether contact lenses are successful or not—certainly, as you indicate, they have been proved successful for quite some time. The purpose of using contact lenses is merely to control visual cues in a developing young animal to provide very critically needed information about the development of vision. Again, may I say that these cats are not uncomfortable, and certainly not in pain through the use of these contact lenses which are ground with precision by the very able researcher in charge of the project.

This kind of experiment is not cruel and certainly is not useless. We know very little about the development of vision and the kinds of experiments that Dr. —————— and others are conducting may provide extremely useful information about sight, hopefully to provide information which would help to correct visual defects and perhaps even to prevent serious defects such as blindness in children. One cannot use human subjects in these experiments largely because the development of the child is much slower than that of the kitten. The kitten, as you know, is fully grown in about a year, developed as an adult, hence the changes in visual acuity and different kinds of perception occur in a manner similar to the human, but at a much more rapid pace, and are more susceptible to careful study.

It is important for laymen to be sufficiently concerned about the welfare of animals and humans in research and to raise their voices in question (and in support); it is also important for them to have enough information to be able to question wisely. In this, the willingness of the scientist to communicate, and the cooperation of news media personnel and scientists, as we will see in the following chapter, is an essential part of the communication of relevant and appropriate information.

Ethical Considerations in Animal Research

Research has been possible only with animals in many crucial areas of science. There are millions of human diabetics in the world today who are alive and have some hope of eventual cure, in large measure because of the original work performed by Banting on dogs. The research scientist follows a rigid code of ethical treatment of experimental animals such as the one established by the National Society for Medical Research. This group includes representatives from such learned societies as the American Psychological Association, the American Medical Association, the Federation of American Societies for Experimental Biology and the American Society for the Prevention of Cruelty to Animals (ASPCA). Here are the six rules established by the American Psychological Association's Committee on Precautions and Standards in Animal Experimentation, in 1962:

1. All animals used for experimental purposes must be lawfully acquired and their retention shall be in strict compliance with Federal and local laws and regulations.
2. Care and feeding of all experimental animals shall be in accordance with accepted laboratory practices, with due consideration for bodily comfort, kind treatment, and sanitary environment.
3. Every effort must be made to avoid unnecessary discomfort to experimental animals. Research subjecting animals to discomfort should be conducted only when an experienced scientist is convinced that such discomfort is required and is justified by the significance of the research.
4. Surgical procedures should be done under suitable anesthesia, and only minor ones under local anesthesia. If the nature of a study is such as to require the animal to survive, acceptable techniques to avoid infection must be followed throughout. If the study does not require survival,

the animal must be disposed of in a humane manner at the conclusion of the operation.

5. The postoperative care of animals must minimize discomfort during convalescence in accordance with accepted practices.

6. When animals are used by students for their education or the advancement of science, such work should be under the direct supervision of an experienced teacher or investigator. The rules for conduct of such work shall be the same as those for the conduct of research.

A copy of these rules shall be posted in all rooms where animals are housed and where animal experimentation is conducted.

Violators of the above rules shall be promptly reported to the director of the laboratory and by him to other administrative authorities if he deems it necessary.

It may be concluded that the most important consideration in doing research with animals, from an ethical standpoint, is the use of standard and acceptable procedures.

Ethical Considerations in Human Research

Over and above the problems of standard ethical research procedures with animals, special considerations arise when the subjects are humans. We strive for reality and control in experiments, and this is directly involved in the problem of ethical design and execution of research. A few years ago, a group of well-trained psychologists in the armed services were upbraided for doing research on stress under simulated combat conditions. One of their experiments went something like this: a recruit was taken into a "combat" area and left in a cave with the instructions that he was to remain in the cave while some blasting went on. He would be protected in the cave from any danger from the explosion. He was equipped with a radio which would receive for him but not transmit. Some time later, there was an explosion. He was told, over the radio, that the explosion had sealed off the entrance to the cave but for him not to worry. Every effort was being taken to get him out. He was told at that time that, if he wished to fix the radio so that it would transmit as well as receive, he should follow instructions. He then received radioed instructions which went along the lines of "take that blue wire leading from the snap lug marked 'C' and run it to the red terminal . . ." and so on, giving him explicit instructions which would make the radio capable of transmitting.

This is an excellent test of the ability to perform a fairly intricate task under stress. To tell him that he was in danger (a stress stimulus) and then to get him to perform a task such as wiring the radio is ingenious—the experimenter could objectively time the moment he radioed the stress stimulus and measure with precision the time elapsed between the radioed stress and the moment the subject came on the air with his own transmission. It is indeed ingenious and realistic as a stress study. It also has carefully controlled variables and, meeting the requirements of a realistic problem and careful variable control, it illustrates an excellent representative design for an experiment. It is, unfortunately, also highly questionable from the standpoint of ethics. The experimenters failed to take into consideration the need for consent by the subject to perform in such an experiment. While it is a good procedure, the risks involved to the health of the subject make it a doubtful one from the standpoint of an acceptable procedure. Inherent in this is the problem of irreversibility of damage. We do not know enough about the effects of stress on a human subject to say that such an experiment would not produce physiological changes that would be permanent and injurious, even without considering the element of risk of fatality which might be a result of severe stress.

This technique of placing a person in a situation in which he believes he is in mortal danger is obviously more effective than asking him how he might behave under such circumstances, or asking him to act out such a situation. The simulation of stress is always a problem. If a study were done in submarines, for example, to test out the effect of living in cramped quarters under difficult conditions for long periods of time, the study would not be valid if the submarine were submerged but moored to a pier, allowing the sailors under study to realize that, in an emergency, they could always surface and get help. The concept of representative design, previously noted, is germane here. Egon Brunswik (32) suggested this term to describe the optimal in experimental design, a minimum of artificiality and a maximum of control over the variables; that is, the problem studied should have reality and yet the variables should be carefully controlled. In this stress situation the question of representative design is important: do you get honest reality and risk lives or produce severe behavioral disruption (as in the case of the cave), or do you sacrifice reality and use less disturbing techniques?

One answer lies in a paper by Irwin Berg (19) in which he spells out the three basic elements of ethical research with human beings: *consent, confidence,* and *standard or acceptable procedure.* First it is necessary always to get the *consent* of the subject in the experiment. "Where the information requested is highly personal or where the experiment involves some pain, discomfort, or risk, the subject should be made fully aware of what he is consenting to, at least in a general way." In the case of patients in psychiatric hospitals it is not always possible or meaningful to gain the consent of a mental patient because he is legally incapable of giving such consent. In such instances, it is possible to get the consent of the patient's physician, his family, or some other person who is responsible for his welfare, before he serves as a subject in a research project. With regard to the use of records, such as hospital records of cases, it is frequently not feasible to get the consent of the patient or the physician. The use of such records in research (or, perhaps, a textbook) is ethical ". . . if the persons concerned are not harmed by the use of their records and their identities are not publicly revealed. . . ."

This relates directly to the second aspect of ethical handling of human subjects, that of *confidence*. No subject would be happy about having others know of his performance on certain tasks or, in the case of questionnaires about personal beliefs, how he responded. If he feels that he can trust the experimenter not to reveal anything about him, he can function more effectively as a subject. The psychologist is bound to the principle of confidence in his work. If he wishes to use the results of a particular study and publish them, he must take care to insure against the identification of any of his subjects. The first two principles, consent and confidence, are illustrated in the well-known Kinsey report on sexual behavior. Kinsey used volunteers in his study of sexual practices—every subject knew exactly the type of questions he would have to answer beforehand and had the opportunity to volunteer or withdraw. In addition, the reports were carefully prepared so that it was not possible for anyone who had participated in the study to be identified. Confidential handling of research data involving human subjects is critical for a relationship of trust between the public and scientist.

The third basic principle governing the use of human subjects in research, as Berg outlines them, is that of *standard* or *acceptable procedure*. This assumes that the experimenter is trained and competent to use procedures in research which his colleagues would accept as standard, that is, "tried many times before by many investigators." Now this poses a special problem, because research obviously cannot use the same procedures over and over again in all cases, if any originality is to occur. In the case of original or novel procedures that are not standard the procedure must be regarded as acceptable by other competent investigators.

There are times when it may be necessary to hide the true purpose of the experiment from the subject. This is always a source of concern to the experimenter. For example, in a well-designed experiment reported by Ralph Hefferline *et al.* (55), the investigators wanted to see if they could condition a subject to make a muscle-twitch response so minute in strength that the subject would be unaware of making it. To record this minute twitch of the thumb, they hooked up an electrode and connected it to an electromyograph which electrically records and amplifies muscle activity. The subjects in the experiment were listening to music and noise was superimposed over the music. They could terminate the noise by the "unconscious" muscle twitch. The subjects were conditioned to this muscle twitch, of which they were unaware, and successfully stopped the unpleasant noise that interfered with their enjoyment of the music. When the subjects were told, in another phase of the experiment, to make a muscle twitch with their thumb to terminate the noise, they were unable to keep the response small enough.

If the subjects had been told originally of the purpose of the experiment, it would have been impossible to find out whether they could be conditioned to an unconscious avoidance response. Knowing the purpose would have made it conscious and, as we see, they were unable to keep the response tiny enough when they consciously tried. This is a novel procedure and, in a sense, the subjects were deceived by the experimenter in his instructions. They consented to an experiment without knowing the exact conditions, but this is not an unethical practice by any stretch of the imagination. The experimenters received a general consent to participate, did not violate the personal privacy of their subjects, subjected them to no discomfort, kept their confidence (although this type of experiment did not concern highly personal responses) and, most important in view of the original nature of the technique, kept to a procedure that would be highly acceptable to all competent psychologists.

These criteria in no way relieve the experimenter of the responsibility for being concerned about deception. No experimenter with human subjects feels completely comfortable in a deception experiment.

Some years ago a competent research psychologist, Evan Pattishall, and I decided to try an experiment to check out universal and personal validation. We were interested in seeing whether descriptive phrases to characterize personality could be so generally vague and universal as to be virtually meaningless. We were also interested in illustrating to students and professionals that meaningless universal terms are not very useful in working with people. We started with an experiment reported by Bertram Forer (47) in which he prepared a personality sketch largely derived from a newsstand book on astrology. Forer administered what he called his "Diagnostic Interest Blank" to an introductory psychology class and told the students that he would give each of them a personality sketch based on the test. The sketches were all identical, but the students did not know it. The sketches consisted of the following items (6):

1. You have a great need for other people to like and admire you.
2. You have a tendency to be critical of yourself.
3. You have a great deal of unused capacity which you have not turned to your advantage.
4. While you have some personality weaknesses, you are generally able to compensate for them.
5. Your sexual adjustment has presented problems for you.
6. Disciplined and self-controlled outside, you tend to be worrisome and insecure inside.
7. At times you have serious doubts as to whether you have made the right decision or done the right thing.
8. You prefer a certain amount of change and variety and become dissatisfied when hemmed in by restrictions and limitations.
9. You pride yourself as an independent thinker and do not accept others' statements without satisfactory proof.

10. You have found it unwise to be too frank in revealing yourself to others.
11. At times you are extroverted, affable, sociable, while at other times you are introverted, wary, reserved.
12. Some of your aspirations tend to be pretty unrealistic.
13. Security is one of your major goals in life.

Forer found that the "adequacy" of the test rated high, and was considered by the students to be a very good personality test. Pattishall and I decided to do a tighter analysis with a more statistical approach, using a standard anxiety scale for credibility. We administered the test to undergraduate and graduate students enrolled in courses in mental hygiene and advanced education psychology, as well as psychiatric residents in training at the University Hospital. The same general approach was taken—that we were going to administer a personality test, then if the individuals wished, we would give them a rating or personality description based upon it. As in the Forer experiment demonstration, the astrology book descriptions were given.

The results were similar to Forer's; most of the subjects felt that the items (except Item 12) were true of themselves and with the exception of Item 6 were also true of other people. More students than psychiatric residents accepted the profile as being characteristic of themselves, but all subjects were about the same in attributing profile characteristics to other people. We believed that this was a good object lesson—that these universal statements illustrated descriptions that were so general as to be useless in analyzing individual subjects.

We did not count upon the ire engendered by the experiment. Indeed, some people said that they were "duped" when it was explained to them that all the personality sketches were identical, and that we were trying to demonstrate universal and personal validation. One psychiatric resident refused to speak to either one of the experimenters from then on, and, in general, a negative feeling occurred in a number of the subjects.

While this feeling diminished somewhat as the hoped-for educational implications of the experiment emerged, it nonetheless constituted a deception experiment with regrettable consequences in interpersonal contact.

As in the Hefferline experiment, not telling the purpose of the experiment was essential to the design but, in both cases, the subjects knew the purpose and results after the conclusion of the studies. Later, this important issue will be discussed further. I would like to concentrate for a moment on the design aspects of experiments in which deception is used. H. C. Kelman (58), in a discussion of deception in human experimentation, cites Martin Orne as observing that the use of deception "on the part of psychologists is so widely known in the college population that even if a psychologist is honest with the subjects, more often than not he will be distrusted." Think what a complex game this might occasion! The student is trying to figure out the "real" purpose of the experiment and act according to his own interpretation of what the experimenter wants, so, as Kelman notes, "the use of deception may actually produce an unspecifiable mixture of intended and unintended stimuli so that it becomes difficult to know exactly what the subject is responding to." A real part of the problem is the possibility that some stimuli might affect the experiment without intent. We know from operant conditioning research that smiles and frowns and nods and glancing at one's watch can alter the rate of verbal behavior (Try looking frequently at your watch while talking to a friend and observe the change!). Is it not possible that such subtly and inadvertently presented stimuli might affect the subject? Take, for example, a study done a few years back by a group of social psychologists who were interested in the behavior of a cult that believed the end of the world was nigh. How would you act if you really believed that the world was coming to an end? (I know some friends who would open up a souvenir stand.) To study this behavior the psychologists joined the cult and professed to share the belief system, manifestly a deception technique. They felt that to come as psychologists openly to study the group would deny them full information, to come as believers would allow them to get inside. To be sure, it was an interesting study with valuable data, but there is a nagging doubt about the ethics of dissembling to the cult and the possibility that unintended cues on the part of the experimenters—facial expressions, postural changes—might somehow have influenced the behavior of the persons studied. The world, by the way, did not end on the date predicted, and the study yielded valuable information about a group disrupted by a belief system that failed.

There are times when deliberate deception is not practiced but the experimenter fails to explain the purpose of the experiment adequately to the subjects, perhaps because he does not think it important or because he assumes that experimental subjects automatically behave as cooperative and relatively passive individuals. An experiment accomplished a few years ago with deep sea divers in a hyperbaric chamber illustrates the risks involved in not cooperating with the subjects. As part of a study to learn about physiological and biochemical change in humans under pressure, a deep sea dive was simulated, and urine specimens were obtained from each diver while in the chamber. No one really sat down and told the divers *why* the data were being gathered, assuming, perhaps, that they would understand the relevance. How the divers themselves might benefit from the research was not explained adequately. It was learned later that the divers passed around the urine bottles and each urinated in all the bottles! (Even confidence-level statistics could not sort out *that* collection; a group urinalysis could not provide accurate P values.) The divers thought it was funny to fool around with the experiment. Had they been included as partners in the research a valuable opportunity for gathering important data might not have been wasted.

In sum, the treatment of the subjects in an experiment as *partners*, not as tools, requires consideration of these crucial steps:

1. The experimenter should carefully explain, as much as is possible and appropriate, the procedures and the purpose of the experiment. Why the data will be of help to the profession and what they will mean to the subject should be covered before the experiment.

2. During the experiment the subject should have a sense of partnership in working with the experimenter. He should be treated courteously and respectfully. I know of one experimenter whose busy schedule often led to delays in or cancellation of experimental runs, inconveniencing the subjects enormously. Subjects are not manila folders.

3. After the experiment the review of the procedure and purpose is imbedded in the results and their meaning. What occurred and what the experiment revealed is of considerable interest to most experimental subjects. Dismissing them summarily without fulfilling their curiosity (which, as you know, is the main motivator to researchers) is discourteous and also misses an opportunity to teach.

With respect to the third point, let me return to the experiment discussed earlier in which universal personality descriptions were given to subjects as their own personality profile. As noted, the debriefing engendered hostility in some subjects, but it was important to the purpose of instructing the subjects (as well as ethical concern) that they be told the exact purpose and results as an object lesson.

Often subjects are not told and are left to wonder about the purpose, and indeed the results, of an experiment. What happens to a research subject *after* an experiment should be a source of concern for any experimenter. Debriefing and explanation of the experiment and what the results meant to the subject is not only courteous, but essential.

This is especially important in experiments with subjects who are going to become professionals. Most psychology students at one time or another are encouraged and expected to participate as subjects in experiments, a main motivation of psychology students—to pick up experience as a subject that will be valuable in later life when they are conducting their own experiments. Too often they are used as subjects without any teaching context. Again, what happens to research subjects after an experiment is a matter of true concern for the experimenter. Research subjects should leave an experiment with a good feeling of what was done, why it was done, its importance—its relevance—what it meant to them as individuals. Otherwise, the subject becomes a tool and no more important than a relay on an electronic rack that might function for the purpose of the experiment.

This leads me to another important ethical consideration of the researcher, the use of research assistants. So far, I have dealt with the research subject, but the assistant who helps in such stages as the preparation, conduct, and analysis of experiments is often neglected. A research assistant often comes in on the middle of an experiment and is programmed to run research—again, almost as though he were a piece of equipment rather than an individual who wants to learn experimental technique. The proper research approach is to treat subjects and assistants as working partners. Then, and only then, can the experimenter maximize the value of the data and serve the important goal of using the research to teach as well.

One final word about acceptable and standard procedures. It is incumbent upon the psychologist conducting research to make absolutely sure that normal precautions are taken in all of his procedures. If he is using electrical apparatus, it is vital that he make certain all wires are properly insulated, equipment is properly grounded, and so on. If the experiment requires physical exertion or stress, it is vital that he have a physician's approval of the physical health of his subject. Normal caution and courtesy will preclude most of the possible problems that might arise in the use of human subjects in research.

The problems discussed so far with regard to research with humans become more critical when research is done using children as experimental subjects. The same principles apply, but it is evident that adults are in a better position to understand the purposes of research and the tasks involved. Certainly an adult would be in a position to consent to experimental procedures, whereas a child would not. The experimenter should therefore gain the consent of the parents of the child, or some responsible related adult, before beginning an experiment. Alfred Baldwin (8) discusses these problems at some length in a handbook on research with children. He points out the necessity for explaining the purposes and plans of research to the parents of children and answering with honesty any questions raised by them. The experimenter cannot allow himself the luxury of considering that the fears of parents are groundless, even though he knows that nothing of potential harm may occur in the course of the research. The experimenter is also enjoined against unnecessary disruption of school or play time for the children in the conduct of the research. The convenience of the subjects should be a major consideration rather than the experimenter's most convenient schedule.

The confidentiality of the material obtained in research with children is as critical as it is with adult subjects, perhaps even more so, because incalculable harm may be done to a child by a well-meaning experimenter who gives parents information about their children that they might not be able to comprehend or use objectively. This is particularly true when the research is conducted by inexperienced experimenters or when the materials used are psychological tests, which are used in research with children as well as adults. This use or misuse of the psychological test also happens in the clinical or school situation, a nonresearch area, and is described by L. J. Stone (95): ". . . There seems to be general recognition of the great fluctuation and low predictive value of individual preschool tests. What is more, so general is the recognition of the doubtful predictive accuracy of an *individual* test, even for older children, that we are much less likely nowadays to find clinicians passing out IQs to parents to be worn like badges of honor or of shame. However, there are still a number of less cautious psychometricians and school testers (often not psychologists) who pass out this kind of unqualified datum far too freely and often produce in this way incalculable damage in the child's picture of himself or in his parents' appraisal of him." This may also apply to results obtained in a nontest research situation.

With both adults and children, the ethical problems of research resolve themselves simply into the humane and considerate practices of interacting with other people. Catherine Landreth, in a letter to the *American Psychologist* published September 1961, invoked the image of Anna in *The King and I*, saying that understanding children and conducting research on them is "largely a matter of: getting to know them, getting to like them, when you are with them getting to know what to say, seeing it their way, as well as putting it your way, but nicely."

Chapter Seven
The Scientist and the Social Order

"Give me a castle on the Rhine, a beautiful girl on an operating table, a hunchback assistant, a roomful of laboratory equipment, and I care not who makes this nation's laws."

—Hans Conreid

The scientist is sometimes pictured in pulp magazines and cheap novels as a fiendish, inhuman, stooped, wild-haired madman whose goal in life is to control the world. The very term "mad scientist" conjures up images of such a figure in a mountaintop laboratory with crackling lights and weird electrical gadgets, and perhaps a few screaming people in large glass bottles waiting for some terrifying experiment. Or perhaps, at the other end of the spectrum, is the image of the absent-minded scientist who forgets his umbrella, bumbles through life dropping acid on his vest (alongside the gravy stains), far from fiendish but equally far from effective.

Both these pictures are arrant nonsense. But with regard to the psychologist in particular, recent years have brought a view of him, in some quarters, as a depth manipulator, a manipulator of men's minds. Packard, in his book *The Hidden Persuaders,* tends to portray some psychologists as invaders of the privacy of our minds. Add to this the concept of brainwashing, and a person is prepared to think that it is possible to control his mind without his being able to resist effectively. Add to this the preparation the public received in other related cases, such as Bridey Murphy, and the impression is reinforced. Elsewhere (4) I have commented:

Packard has left us with a term quite as dramatic and chilling as brainwashing—he has referred to motivation researchers as "depth manipulators," a term bound to fall on fertile soil prepared for the public by the "depth manipulation" of the magical unconscious as demonstrated in the *Three Faces of Eve* or the hypnotic control in the highly publicized *Search for Bridey Murphy*. To be sure, the psychologist is critical of such events. He may offer alternative explanations to the "multiple personality" of Eve, and he may point out the falsities in Bridey Murphy's mysterious "reincarnation." But, after the clear thinking is over, there remains in the public mind the salient thought that the person has an unconscious unknown even to himself, he has no conscious control of this (an idea reinforced in the *Three Faces of Eve,* where "personalities struggled with each other for control"), and someone else, through brainwashing or hypnosis, can control him.

These are problems in what has been referred to as the public image of the psychologist—what people think of him and his work. While far from strongly entrenched, such beliefs about the mad scientist or "depth manipulator" qualities of the psychologist do him an injustice and are a disservice to science in general.

The Scientist's Communication to the Public

The necessity for operational definitions in science (Chapters 3 and 4) produces special problems in the communication of the scientist's work to nonscientific audiences. A common ground must be achieved between the technical language of science and the nontechnical language of everyday life. This conversion must be accomplished in such a way, however, as not to misrepresent the technical statement. This is a difficult task, and often, as a result, many magazines simply do not bother to insure a complete equivalence of meaning.

Speak to any scientist and you are likely to find a man who has been burned by popularization. Newspapers in our culture are not designed to be purveyors of scientific information. They are primarily a source of entertainment and news. Where scientific information generally appears (except in such papers as *The New York Times*) is in the rotogravure section of the Sunday paper, manifestly not a news section but rather an entertainment folio. Popular news sources tend to give the reader a capsule education in science, which is often a deceptively simple account of relativity theory or medical research. For example, there are the popularized accounts of drugs that produce psychotic-like states, accounts that read something like "Cary Grant's New Soul Through The Miracle Mind Drug, Lysergic Acid."

So alongside a story of Italian movie starlets, perhaps a rehash of the disappearance of Judge Crater, recipes for Thanksgiving, and the favorite jokes of a TV comic, will appear something about science, usually couched in a mystique peculiar to such popularization with standard words such as "miracle," "wonder," and "marvel" underscoring the inevitably "new" breakthrough of science. The researcher whose preliminary work on a prosthetic device for amputees is written up in a popular magazine under a title such as "Science Brings New Hope to the Amputee," in which an account of a "miraculous" new artificial hand is splashed in color, is not fairly or adequately represented.

A friend of mine had this very thing happen to him. A widely circulated weekly magazine heard about his laboratory's work on this new artificial hand and asked to write it up. His understanding was that it would be an account of a preliminary nature on the experimental work that had gone into researching and developing the prosthetic device. Instead, it was told as a *fait accompli*, a miracle wrought in the laboratory. One tragic consequence of such irresponsible handling of the story was a deluge of phone calls to the laboratory and clinic where the device was being developed. Irate and disillusioned veterans, amputees who had been treated at the clinic, demanded to know why this new miracle had been kept from them. It was a hard job explaining that the device was still in the early stages of research. It is this sort of experience that so often sours researchers on communication of information to the layman.

The perception of the scientist by the layman is often distorted in such a fashion, and yet it is impossible for a scientist not to be touched by the social impact of his research in some fashion. As I have noted in another paper (5):

. . . the scientist has been considered something like a servant god, offered homage but expected to produce miracles on command. And, as with all inefficient gods, the shamanistic scientist is often excoriated and repudiated by his people, a fact which may make the scientist even less interested in leaving his laboratory and assuming his social responsibility. It is inevitable that a scientific discovery ultimately is expressed as social change and it is equally inevitable that the scientist must eventually perceive his work in a social context.

In recent years, the support available for scientific research has increased markedly, particularly with the growth of funds appropriated by the federal government as well as private foundations. With this increased support, however, there is a curious conviction held by many people that money is the answer to scientific searches. This may be related to what I have referred to above as the Shamanistic quality of the scientist—as a magician he should be able to perform miracles, given enough money. The cure for cancer is one of the truly critical problems of our time, and the search for a solution to this disease requires money for apparatus, laboratories, and scientific personnel to carry on the research. But neither money nor the ability of dedicated scientists is *sufficient*, although each is *necessary*. For in addition to money and dedicated research in any one field, every science depends upon other scientists for new breakthroughs of information—for example, the electron microscope opened up new sources of information for neurology, and electronic computers made data processing possible as never before. With an advance in one science, then, progress *may* be made in others, but this is at best an uneven development. The search for a cure for cancer may come unexpectedly from a laboratory working on problems of virus disorders, or from other scientists whose efforts are not immediately directed toward this special research area. It is necessary to integrate many factors before a "breakthrough" is possible. Selig Hecht discusses this with regard to the development of the atomic bomb (54):

> We should know that all the money in the world could not have built an atomic bomb in 1936. Atomic energy was known, and many of its properties were understood. It had been released in small quantities in laboratories, and its release in large quantities in the sun and the stars had been studied. But the critical information and the critical direction to follow for releasing it in large amounts on earth were lacking in 1936, and no one could have used two billion dollars for making an atomic bomb at that time. It is this that is important in understanding the relation of science to industry, to medicine, and to the public. There has to be knowledge before it can be applied. At a certain stage of scientific development, theoretically critical knowledge becomes available. Before that moment—which no one can guarantee in advance—the knowledge cannot be applied. After that moment application is reasonably certain and only the special technics for its utilization need be worked out.

I have described the negative side of communication to the laity only to explain why so many scientists are reluctant to present research information for popular consumption. There is, fortunately, another side to the story, found in highly responsible science writers, newspapers, and magazines. These individuals and media of communication represent what the French have called *haute vulgarisation* (literally, high-level vulgarization). They attempt to present scientific information in a manner comprehensible to the intelligent layman and as comprehensively as possible without doing injury to the information. Magazines such as *Scientific American* serve such a purpose extremely well. There are many excellent science writers who try to balance accuracy with interesting writing. Among these are such fine authors as John Pfeiffer, Michael Amrine, and Daniel Greenberg, and Loren Eisely, a scientist himself.

There is no doubt that the scientist has a responsibility for the communication of his research, first to his colleagues, next to the public. Ernest Renan, in 1848, wrote:

The specialist-*savant,* far from deserting the true arena of humanity, is the one who labours most efficaciously to the progress of the intellect, seeing that he alone can provide us with the materials for its constructions. But his researches cannot have an aim in themselves, for they do not contribute to make the author more perfect, they are of no value until they are introduced into the grand current.

This is echoed by Jean Rostand in 1960, who observed that "the ideal of the popularization of science (and here lies its moral value) is to develop and assist a community of thought."

The Scientist's Communication to Other Scientists

The necessity for communication among scientists is, perhaps, of even greater importance than is the communication of scientific information to the public. Throughout the book, there have been references to the manner in which most scientific communication takes place through journals, books, papers presented at scientific meetings, and informal social contact. There are journals limited in large measure to the specific subject matter of the science, such as the *Journal of the Experimental Analysis of Behavior,* the *Journal of Comparative and Physiological Psychology,* and the *American Psychologist* in the field of psychology, *Nuclear Physics, The Journal of the Optical Society of America,* and the *Journal of Biochemistry,* to name some examples from other scientific disciplines. Scientists tend to publish in their own discipline's journals or in journals that reach an audience of similar interests; for example, a psychologist working in the area of vision research might well publish in the *Journal of the Optical Society of America,* or, perhaps, a biochemist engaged in research on brain chemistry might submit his writings to the journal *Experimental Neurology.* There are, in addition, several journals of a more catholic scientific audience such as the magazine *Scientific American,* in which scientists in varying disciplines can write for each other in a manner comprehensible also to the nonscientist. Another weekly journal, *Science,* published by the American Association for the Advancement of Science, reports research of a technical nature as well as theoretical papers from all sciences in addition to reports of political and public affairs of interest to the scientific community. Now as never before, there is an immense amount of available literature in science. This in itself creates a significant problem for the scientist, who cannot easily keep up with the spate of material pouring forth in journals. In recent years, this problem has been attacked as an exercise in data storage and retrieval through the use of computers, but for the everyday reading of the average scientist a necessary compromise must be made with the ideal of reading everything. He selects perhaps a few journals to read with regularity, scans abstracts of published literature and depends to some degree upon his colleagues to mention papers he might have missed.

What happens to research when it is published? It is probable, for one thing, that those individuals who have a special interest in the area covered by the research will evaluate the report in terms of their own experience, particularly if it departs from other findings in a significant manner. Readers will be likely to examine the data and the design of the research with a highly critical eye to see if any flaws in the research may gainsay the results. It is important, as we have seen in discussing operational approaches to research (p. 81 ff.), for the experimenter to specify clearly what he has done so that another experimenter may replicate his experiment if he wishes.

As a body of literature grows in a particular area, the interest of researchers is stimulated and different aspects of the area come under more intensive study. As a body of information is developed and the evidence for or against a certain concept or theory piles up, researchers become convinced that one approach is better than another, or that certain sets of facts indicate that Condition A is in effect instead of Conditions B or C. Although ideally this process occurs with complete impartiality, with the integrity and rationality so prized as the hallmarks of scientific research, nevertheless a human tendency to wish that one were right despite the evidence sometimes develops. When this occurs, the resistance of scientists to the communication of others cannot help but affect the dissemination of information and its application. Earlier (page 37) we have referred to the "pig-headed orthodoxy of science" to describe the tendency of scientists to resist new and different information, at the same time indicating that such a resistance was necessary in the interests of time, for qualified scientists cannot be expected to take time to disprove every theory, crackpot or not, that comes along. As I suggested before, it is up to the innovator to prove his point while it is the responsibility of the community of science to listen. Thus the established scientific community must be as open-minded as the discoverer or innovator is reputable. The reputation of the experimenter is of prime importance in the evaluation of data, for as Sidman (83) notes:

. . . no experimental data are independent of the experimenter. His past and present experiments are not independent of each other. The experimenter constitutes a thread of correlation running through them all, a correlation arising not from the experimenter's physical presence or from his name, but from his techniques of experimental control.

Given the integrity of the scientist and the necessity for some resistance in the interests of time, why are there occasions when scientists resist challenging data? Barber (9), in an article on the history of scientific resistance to discovery, distinguishes several types of cultural resistance. One of these is that of *preconceived substantive conceptions and theories* which often hinder discoveries. Even in the most industrious and talented of scientists this form of resistance can occur, as we have seen in "The Case of the Floppy-Eared Rabbits" discussed in Chapter 1.

Religious beliefs may also play a role. Whenever one thinks of conflicts between scientific and religious belief it is usual to emphasize the position of the religious layman or theologian who resists ideas contrary to a religious system, but it is also possible for a scientist who is deeply religious to resist theories or data that may challenge his own beliefs. A Victorian scientist, for example, who was devoutly religious might be expected to resist a theory such as Darwin's, which challenged his beliefs regarding the origins of man.

Barber lists still another source of possible resistance in the *social interaction of scientists*: as he observes (10):

In general, higher professional standing in science is achieved by the more competent, those who have demonstrated their capacity for being creative in their own right and for judging the discoveries of others. But sometimes, when discoveries are made by scientists of lower standing, they are resisted by scientists of higher standing partly because of the authority the higher position provides.

The monk Mendel was ignored for many years because of his

lack of professional standing; the scientific societies then in existence were not interested in this nonscientist's quaint ideas about genetics.

For the most part, examples of resistance to scientific discovery occur in the nineteenth century or earlier. Barber, for example, refers to the difficulties experienced by Faraday, Galton, Lavoisier, and Copernicus, among others, but these were scientists challenging established thought in a time of somewhat limited communication.

Resistance can and certainly does happen today, but I believe it is much less likely because of the very nature of science as it has developed, from a rather limited and aristocratic pursuit —a gentleman's avocation perhaps—to a truly democratic system in which opportunity for status and success are mainly contingent upon ability. It is nevertheless a tendency to guard against vigorously. Barber summarizes the problem (11):

> That some resistance occurs, that it has specifiable sources in culture and social interaction, that it may be in some measure inevitable, is not proof either that there is more resistance than acceptance in science or that scientists are no more open-minded than other men. On the contrary, the powerful norm of open-mindedness in science, the objective tests by which concepts and theories often can be validated, and the social mechanisms for ensuring competition among ideas new and old—all these make up a social system in which objectivity is greater than it is in other social areas, resistance less. The development of modern science demonstrates this ever so clearly. Nevertheless, some resistance remains, and it is this we seek to understand and thus perhaps to reduce. . . . As men in society, scientists are sometimes the agents, sometimes the objects, of resistance to their own discoveries.

In summary, then, there must be a balance in scientific communication to other scientists, just as there must be a balance in communication to the general public. The community of scientists should be neither closed, resulting in oligarchism, nor completely open, resulting in anarchism. As Bronowski (29) has stated:

> The society of scientists must be a democracy. It can keep alive and grow only by a constant tension between dissent and respect, between independence from the views of others and tolerance for them. The crux of the ethical problem is to fuse these, the private and the public needs.

In its own society, which is a replica in miniature of the larger society of which modern science is both the agent and the product, scientists are no more than citizens, sharing a common culture; however, care should be taken that they are no less than scientists, following that special (and specialized) tradition indicated by Bronowski (30) of independence, originality, and as a product of these qualities, dissent.

It is absolutely imperative for scientists to communicate their knowledge as well as they can, accepting the social responsibility of education suggested by Renan and Rostand and by the Archbishop of York, who once told the British Association for the Advancement of Science that scientists "must educate their fellow countrymen to use rightly the inventions they have given them, and must make plain the terrifying results which may follow their wrong use."

It is easy enough to see the relevance of the Archbishop's statement to nuclear physics and the threat of annihilation, but it is also relevant to psychology. In an address before the American Psychological Association in 1955, the brilliant physicist Robert Oppenheimer made the following observation about physics and psychology:

> In the last ten years the physicists have been extraordinarily noisy about the immense powers which, largely through their efforts, but through other efforts as well, have come into the

possession of man, powers notably and strikingly for very large-scale and dreadful destruction. We have spoken of our responsibilities and of our obligations to society in terms that sound to me very provincial, because the psychologist can hardly do anything without realizing that for him the acquisition of knowledge opens up the most terrifying prospects of controlling what people do and how they think and how they behave and how they feel. This is true for all of you who are engaged in practice, and as the corpus of psychology gains in certitude and subtlety and skill, I can see that the physicist's pleas that what he discovers be used with humanity and be used wisely will seem rather trivial compared to those pleas which you will have to make and for which you have to be responsible.

Science and the Social Order

In the last chapter the section dealing with ethical considerations was concerned, for the most part, with ethical procedures in the design and execution of research. Because the ethical concerns experienced by scientists in research are based on social responsibility, it may be of value to examine the ethics of the scientist with respect to the social system in which he works and lives. Science, as universal a realm as music, is affected as equally as music by the culture in which it develops.

How does one evaluate a culture? One effective way is to examine the particular characteristics of a society that distinguishes it from other societies. Kingsley Davis (41), for example, has delineated the characteristics of our own open-class society in a sociological analysis of the ethical system it has developed. This open-class ethic, he indicates, is:

1. *Democratic* in the sense of favoring equal opportunity to rise socially by merit rather than by birth.
2. *Worldly* in emphasizing earthly values such as the pursuit

of a calling, accumulation of wealth, and achievement of status.

3. But at the same time *ascetic* in stressing physical abstinence and stern sobriety, thrift, industry, and prudence.

4. *Individualistic* in placing responsibility on the individual himself for his economic, political and religious destiny, and in stressing personal ambition, self-reliance, private enterprise, and entrepreneurial ability.

5. *Rationalistic* and *empirical* in assuming a world order discoverable through sensory observation of nature.

6. *Utilitarian* in pursuing practical ends with the best available means, and conceiving human welfare in secularized terms as attainable by human knowledge and action.

Davis suggests that such an ethical system is functionally related to an open-class society such as ours. It is also obvious that the characteristics of such an ethical code are part and parcel of the science that has developed within our society; the emphasis on truth, industry, reason, and integrity so prized in our culture reach fruition in its scientific expression. Science as a system has adopted the ethics and values of the society, and has in turn contributed importantly towards the development and practice of these ethics and values. It is perhaps also true that science is somewhat ahead of the society in its emphasis on the individual. Integrity is not an abstraction in science—it is a crucial aspect of the everyday behavior of each scientist as a person. As such, the individual elements tend to personalize and humanize the abstract code of ethics. As Bronowski has observed (31):

. . . like the other creative activities which grew from the Renaissance, science has humanized our values. Men have asked for freedom, justice and respect precisely as the scientific spirit has spread among them. The dilemma of today is not that the human values cannot control a mechanical science. It is the other way about: the scientific spirit is more human than the machinery of governments. . . . Our conduct as states clings to a code of self-interest which science, like humanity, has long left behind. The body of technical science burdens and threatens us because we are trying to employ the body without the spirit, we are trying to buy the corpse of science.

Hermann Bondi (20) has discussed the human qualities of scientific endeavors. Emphasizing in particular the need for testing to counter human fallibility, he suggests that science, more than any other enterprise, reckons with human error, "because anybody may be wrong, it is pointless to refer to authority, for great scientists can be no less wrong than others . . . it is through this insistence on checking that science has become universal" (21). Theories must be worked out so that they may be testable, so that people may work together to build knowledge. It is especially this quality of working together that makes for the humanized science of which Bronowski and Bondi speak. Bondi goes on to observe (22):

Not long ago a history don wrote in an educational journal that he felt that, since present problems were largely problems of human relations, an education in the humanities, which dealt with human beings, fitted people better for this world than an education in science, which dealt with facts. This statement is nonsense. Science is a human endeavor and, moreover, it is the human endeavor in which world wide co-operation has been more successful than in any other. It is a human endeavor singularly well tailored to human abilities and human failings. If anything can teach you to co-operate with other human beings, irrespective of race or religion, ideology or nationality, then it is science. In this sense it is perhaps a far more human subject than the so-called humanities, and to speak about it as dealing impersonally, solitarily, with facts is so gross a misunderstanding of what science is, that it comes as a shock to realize that such views can still be held.

To say, as Bondi does, that science is sometimes misunderstood is not to plead for some vague, uncritical acceptance by the nonscientist, but rather to indicate the responsibility of the nonscientist to make a genuine attempt to comprehend. The history don to whom Bondi refers renders, as a layman outside of science, uncritical judgment, for it is his responsibility to understand science and scientists, just as we have seen it is the scientist's responsibility to make himself understood.

One of the purposes of this little book, besides introducing some information about scientific methodology, is to acquaint the nonscientist with some characteristics of the scientist and the scientific life. It can be no more than an introduction to the rigor, the flexibility, the fun and the frustration, the mechanics and the humanity of research.

Bibliography

1. Arnold, Magda. *Emotions and Personality, Vol I.* New York: Columbia University Press, 1960, p. 143.
2. Asimov, Isaac. *The Intelligent Man's Guide to Science, Vol. I: The Physical Sciences.* New York: Basic Books, 1960, p. 290.
3. Bachrach, Arthur J. (ed.). *Experimental Foundations of Clinical Psychology.* New York: Basic Books, 1962.
4. Bachrach, Arthur J. "The Ethics of Tachistoscopy," *Bulletin of the Atomic Scientists,* 5 (May 1959), 212–215.
5. *Ibid.,* p. 214.
6. Bachrach, Arthur J., and Evan G. Pattishall. "An Experiment in Universal and Personal Validation," *Psychiatry: Journal for the Study of Interpersonal Processes,* 23 (August 1960), 267–270.
7. Bachrach, Arthur J., Frank W. Banghart, and Evan G. Pattishall. "Comments on the Diagnostician as Computer," *Neuropsychiatry,* 6 (Fall 1960), 32.
8. Baldwin, Alfred L. "The Study of Child Behavior and Development," in Paul H. Mussen (ed.), *Handbook of Research Methods in Child Development.* New York: Wiley, 1960, Chap. 1, pp. 3–35.
9. Barber, Bernard. "Resistance by Scientists to Scientific Discovery," *Science,* 134 (September 1, 1961), 596–602.
10. *Ibid.,* pp. 4–5.
11. *Ibid.,* pp. 6–7.
12. Barber, Bernard, and Renee C. Fox. "The Case of the Floppy-Eared Rabbits: An Instance of Serendipity Gained and Serendipity Lost," *American Journal of Sociology,* 54 (September 1958), 128–136. Quoted by permission of The University of Chicago Press. Copyright 1958 by The University of Chicago.
13. *Ibid.,* p. 130.
14. *Ibid.,* p. 131.
15. *Ibid.,* p. 132.
16. *Ibid.,* p. 134.
17. *Ibid.,* p. 135.

18. Belousov, V. V. "Experimental Geology," *Scientific American*, 204 (February 1961), 96–106.

19. Berg, Irwin A. "The Use of Human Subjects in Psychological Research," *American Psychologist*, 9 (March 1954), 108–111.

20. Bondi, Hermann. "Why Scientists Talk," in *The Language of Science*. New York: Basic Books, 1963, pp. 19–38.

21. *Ibid.*, p. 25.

22. *Ibid.*, p. 25.

23. Brady, Joseph V. "Emotional Behavior," in John Field, V. E. Hall, and H. W. Magoun (eds.), *Handbook of Physiology. Section I., Neurophysiology Vol. III.* American Physiological Society, 1959, p. 1529.

24. Bridgman, Percy W. *The Intelligent Individual and Society.* New York: Macmillan, 1938.

25. Bronowski, Jacob. *The Common Sense of Science.* Cambridge, Mass.: Harvard University Press, 1953, p. 70.

26. *Ibid.*, p. 130.

27. *Ibid.*, p. 131.

28. Bronowski, Jacob. *Science and Human Values.* New York: Harper & Row, 1959, p. 67.

29. *Ibid.*, p. 80.

30. *Ibid.*, pp. 77–78.

31. *Ibid.*, pp. 90–91.

32. Brunswik, Egon. "The Conceptual Framework of Psychology," *International Encyclopedia of Unified Sciences*, 6 (1952), 659–751.

33. Bustad, L. K. "The Experimental Subject—A Choice Not an Echo," *Perspectives in Biology and Medicine*, Vol. 14 (Autumn 1970).

34. *Canadian Medical Association Journal* (December 28, 1968), pp. 1266–1267.

35. Cannon, Walter B. *The Way of An Investigator.* New York: Norton, 1945.

36. Chase, Stuart. *The Tyranny of Words.* New York: Harcourt, Brace, 1938, p. 21.

37. *Ibid.*

38. *Ibid.*, p. 380.

39. Cohen, Robert S., quoted in M. W. Wartofsky, *Conceptual Foundations of Scientific Thought: An Introduction to the Philosophy of Science.* New York: Macmillan, 1968, p. 414.

40. Copeland, Paul L., and William E. Bennett. *Elements of Modern Physics.* New York: Oxford University Press, 1961, p. 57.

41. Davis, Kingsley. "Mental Hygiene and the Class Structure," in

A. Rose (ed.), *Mental Health and Mental Disorder.* New York: Norton, 1955, p. 580.

42. Davis, R. C. "Physical Psychology," *Psychological Review,* 60 (1953), 7–14.

43. de Ford, Charles S., quoted in Martin Gardner, *Fads and Fallacies in the Name of Science.* New York: Dover, 1957, p. 12.

44. *Diagnostic and Statistical Manual of Mental Disorders.* Washington, D.C.: American Psychiatric Association, 1952.

45. English, Oliver S., and Stuart M. Finch. *Introduction to Psychiatry.* New York: Norton, 1954.

46. Feigl, Herbert. "Operationism and Scientific Method," *Psychological Review,* Vol. 52 (1945).

47. Forer, Bertram R. "The Fallacy of Personal Validation: A Classroom Demonstration of Gullibility," *Journal of Abnormal and Social Psychology,* 14 (1949), 118–123.

48. Freud, Anna. *The Ego and the Mechanisms of Defense.* New York: International Universities, 1948, p. 43.

49. Gardner, Martin. "Dermo-Optical Perception: A Peek Down the Nose," *Science,* 151 (February 11, 1966), 654–657.

50. Gardner, Martin. *Fads and Fallacies in the Name of Science.* New York: Dover, 1957, p. 30.

51. *Ibid.,* p. 11.

52. Walter, W. G. *The Living Brain.* New York: Norton, 1953, p. 33.

53. Greenspoon, Joel. "Private Experience Revisited," *Psychological Record,* 11 (1961), 373–381.

54. Hecht, Selig. *Exploring the Atom.* New York: Viking, 1948, p. 7.

55. Hefferline, Ralph F., B. Keenan, and R. A. Harford. "Escape and Avoidance Conditioning in Human Subjects Without Their Observation of the Response," *Science,* 130 (1959), 1338–1339.

56. Hull, Clark L. "Hypothetico-Deductive Method of Theory Construction," in L. Stolurow (ed.), *Readings in Learning.* Englewood Cliffs, N.J.: Prentice-Hall, 1953, pp. 9–30.

57. Ivan, L. T. "Irreversible Brain Damage and Related Problems: Pronouncement of Death," *Journal of the American Geriatrics Society,* 18 (1970), 816–822.

58. Kelman, H. C. "The Human Use of Human Subjects: The Problem of Deception in Social-Psychological Experiments," paper delivered at the seventy-third annual convention of the American Psychological Association, Chicago, 1965.

59. Kluckhohn, Clyde. "Culture and Behavior," in Gardner Lindzey (ed.), *Handbook of Social Psychology, Vol. II.* Cambridge, Mass.: Addison Wesley, 1954, p. 938.

60. Kluckhohn, F. R. "Dominant and Substitute Profiles of Cultural

Orientations: Their Significance for the Analysis of Social Stratification," *Social Forces*, 28 (May 1950), 376–393.

61. Kuhn, T. *The Structure of Scientific Revolutions.* Chicago: University of Chicago Press, 1962.

62. *Ibid.,* p. 10.

63. *Ibid.,* p. 159.

64. *Ibid.,* p. 166.

65. Margenau, Henry. "Philosophical Problems in Physics," in Charles W. Churchman and Philburn Ratoosh (eds.), *Measurement: Definition and Theories.* New York: Wiley, 1959, pp. 167ff.

66. Marx, Melvin H. "The General Nature of Theory Construction," in Melvin Marx (ed.), *Psychological Theory.* New York: Macmillan, 1950, pp. 7–8.

67. Masserman, Jules H. *Principles of Dynamic Psychiatry.* Philadelphia: Saunders, 1961.

68. Pronko, N. H. "A Classroom Demonstration of Extrasensory Perception," *Psychological Record,* 11 (1961), 423–426.

69. Quine, Willard. "Truth by Convention," in *Philosophical Essays for Alfred North Whitehead.* New York: Longmans Green, 1946.

70. Rapoport, Anatol. *Operational Philosophy.* New York: Harper and Bros., 1954, p. 74.

71. Rapoport, Anatol. "What Is Semantics?" *American Scientist,* 40 (1952), 123–135.

72. Reichenbach, Hans. *Experience and Prediction.* Chicago: University of Chicago Press, 1938.

73. Renan, Ernest. *The Future of Science,* 1848.

74. Ryle, Gilbert. *The Concept of Mind.* New York: Macmillan, 1950.

75. Sidman, Murray. *Tactics of Scientific Research.* New York: Basic Books, 1960, p. 15. Quoted by permission of Basic Books, Inc.

76. *Ibid.,* p. 9.

77. *Ibid.,* p. 13.

78. *Ibid.,* p. 17.

79. *Ibid.,* pp. 20–21.

80. *Ibid.,* p. 27.

81. *Ibid.,* p. 27.

82. *Ibid.,* p. 28.

83. *Ibid.,* p. 80.

84. Sidman, Murray. "Verplanck's Analysis of Skinner," *Contemporary Psychology,* 1 (January 1956), 8.

85. Skinner, B. F. "A Case History in Scientific Method," in *Cumulative Record.* New York: Macmillan, 1956, p. 81.

86. Skinner, B. F. *Science and Human Behavior.* New York: Macmillan, 1953, p. 13.

87. *Ibid.,* p. 12.
88. *Ibid.,* p. 12.
89. *Ibid.,* p. 13.
90. *Ibid.,* p. 13.
91. *Ibid.,* pp. 38–39.
92. Skinner, B. F. *Verbal Behavior.* New York: Appleton-Century-Crofts, 1957, pp. 8–9.
93. Stevens, S. S. "Psychology and the Science of Science," *Psychological Bulletin,* Vol. 36 (1939).
94. Stevenson, Ian P. *The Evidence for Survival From Claimed Memories of Former Incarnations.* Surrey, Eng.: M. C. Peto, 1961. (Originally published in the *Journal of the American Society for Psychical Research,* April and July 1960.)
95. Stone, L. J. "Recent Developments in Diagnostic Testing of Children," in *Recent Advances in Diagnostic Psychological Testing.* Springfield, Mass.: Thomas, 1950, pp. 82–83.
96. Strupp, H. H. "Patient-Doctor Relationships: The Psychotherapist in the Therapeutic Processes," in Arthur J. Bachrach (ed.), *Experimental Foundations of Clinical Psychology.* New York: Basic Books, 1962.
97. Underwood, B. J. *Psychological Research.* New York: Appleton-Century-Crofts, 1957, p. 19.
98. Wartofsky, M. W. *Conceptual Foundations of Scientific Thought: An Introduction to the Philosophy of Science.* New York: Macmillan, 1968.
99. Weber, Max. *The Methodology of the Social Sciences.* Glencoe, Ill.: Free Press, 1949.
100. Wenger, Marion, F. N. Jones, and M. H. Jones. *Physiological Psychology.* New York: Holt, Rinehart and Winston, 1956.
101. Young, J. Z. *Doubt and Certainty in Science.* Oxford: Clarendon Press, 1951, pp. 1–2.

Suggested Further Reading

In addition to many of the books referred to in the Bibliography, there are some volumes that may prove of interest to readers who wish to go into some more detailed and advanced analyses of scientific method and research. The following list offers a varied group of such volumes:

Bernard, C. *An Introduction to the Study of Experimental Medicine.* New York: Collier Books, 1961.

Beveridge, W. I. B. *The Art of Scientific Investigation.* New York: Vintage Books, 1957.

Brunswik, Egon. *The Conceptual Framework of Psychology.* Chicago: University of Chicago Press, 1952.

Cannon, W. *The Way of An Investigator.* New York: Norton, 1945.

Edel, A. *The Theory and Practice of Philosophy.* New York: Harcourt, Brace, 1946.

Foucalt, Michel. *The Order of Things: An Archaeology of the Human Sciences.* London: Tavistock, 1970.

Frank, Philipp. *Modern Science and Its Philosophy.* Cambridge, Mass.: Harvard University Press, 1949.

Freedman, P. *The Principles of Scientific Research.* 2nd ed. New York: Pergamon Press, 1960.

Hall, A. R., and M. B. Hall. *A Brief History of Science.* New York: Signet, 1964.

Jørgensen, Jørgen. *The Development of Logical Empiricism.* Chicago: University of Chicago Press, 1951.

Kaplan, Abraham. *The Conduct of Inquiry: Methodology for Behavioral Sciences.* San Francisco: Chandler, 1964.

Koch, Sigmund (ed.). *Psychology: A Study of a Science.* New York: McGraw-Hill, 1959 forward, 7 volumes.

Marx, M. H., and W. A. Hillix. *Systems and Theories in Psychology.* New York: McGraw-Hill, 1963.

Osgood, C. E. *Method and Theory in Experimental Psychology.* New York: Oxford University Press, 1953.

Psychological Abstracts. Washington: American Psychological Association, since 1927, bimonthly.

Reichenbach, H. *The Rise of Scientific Philosophy.* Berkeley: University of California Press, 1951.

Selye, Hans. *From Dream to Discovery: On Being a Scientist.* New York: McGraw-Hill, 1964.

Stevens, S. S. (ed.). *Handbook of Experimental Psychology.* New York: Wiley, 1951.

Woodworth, R. S., and Harold Scholsberg. *Experimental Psychology.* Rev. ed. New York: Holt, Rinehart and Winston, 1954 [1938].

Index

Accidental discoveries, 15, 20
American Psychiatric Association, *Diagnostic Manual*, 82
American Psychologist, 121
Amontons, Guillaume, 56
Amrine, Michael, 127
Analogue error, 95–99
Animal research, 92–95; ethical aspects, 15, 108–109; reasons for, 92–93; selection of animals, 93–95
Anxiety, 78–79
Apparatus design, 18, 71–72
Armadillos, use in research, 94
Arnold, Magda, 65
Asimov, Isaac, 55–56
Astrology book, 114–115
Astronomy, 38
Atomic bomb, 126

Bachrach, Arthur J., 114–115, 122–123, 125
Bacon, Roger, 39
Baldwin, Alfred L., 120
Barber, Bernard, 25–32, 130–131
Behavior, animal and human, 70, 72–73, 91–95; avoidance, 72; definitions, 78–81; describing, 52; drugs and, 72–73; measurement of, 54; study of, 36; verbal, 23–24
Bennett, William E., 34
Berg, Irwin A., 111–112
Bondi, Hermann, 135–136
Boyle, Robert, 56
Brady, Joseph V., 65
Brain, study of, 92–93

Bridgman, Percy W., 82
Bronowski, Jacob, 39–40, 47–48, 91, 132, 134–135
Brunswik, Egon, 89, 111
Bustad, L. K., 93

Canadian Medical Association, 104
Cannon, Walter B., 20
Careful casual, 19–21
Cats and dogs, use of in research, 93
Celsius, Anders, 57
Chase, Stuart, 76
Children, research using, 120–121
Clocks, 57–58, 86
Cohen, Robert, 100, 102
Communication, scientific, 63, 123–132
Concepts, inferred and invented, 87–88
Conreid, Hans, 122
Control of data, 38, 50, 52, 71–73
Conventions, scientific, 25
Copeland, Paul L., 34
Culture, evaluating characteristics, 133–134
Curiosity of scientists, 15–19

Data, scientific, 15, 34–38; collection of, 16; consistent terminology
    for, 83; control of, 38, 50, 52, 71–73; establishment of functional
    relationships of, 16; inferred and invented concepts of, 87–88;
    meaning of, 16; respect for, 35; subjective phenomena of, 54;
    theory construction of, 59–73
Darwin, Charles, 23
Data language, 41
Davis, Kingsley, 133–134
Davis, R. C., 42
Death, defining, 104
Deception, in research, 113–117
Decision making, 60–61
Deductive process, 60–62
Definition of terms, 74–88; certainty and clarity, 74–86; daily, 77; opera-
    tional, 16, 81–86; phenomena or events, 74; poetic, 77; problem of,
    74–88; scientific, 77–81; specificity, 77; three levels of, 77–78; vari-
    ables, 74; verbal symbolic terms, 86

de Ford, Charles S., 46
Depression, study of, 96
Dermo-optical perception, 44
Descartes, René, 39
Description, 38, 52; levels of, 53
Dictionary definitions, 73–74
Discussions, informal among scientists, 23–25

Economy, principles of, 63–64
Einstein, Albert, 34, 40, 43
Eisley, Loren, 127
Emotion, definition of, 83–84; research on, 54; theories of, 65
Ethical aspects of research, 100–109, 133–135; animal research, 108–109; human research, 109–121
Experimentation, 37, 35–39, 46–50; analogue error, 95–99; control of data, 68–73; controlled procedures, 62; design, 89, 110–111; manipulation, 52, 63, 71; negative results of, 28, 34–35; prediction from, 49–52; presentation of results, 34; reason from, 46–49; replication, 41; representative design, 89, 110–111; toward order and law, 46–49; variability, 41–43
Extrasensory perception (ESP), 42–45

Facts, acceptance of in science, 36–37
Fahrenheit, Gabriel, 56–57
Feigl, Herbert, 88
FitzGerald, G. F., 34
Fleming, Sir Alexander, 16–17, 20
Floppy-eared rabbits, case of, 25–32
Forer, Bertram, 114–115
Fox, Renée C., 25–32

Galileo, 33, 55
Gardner, Martin, 36, 44–46
Geology, 38
Goals of science, 38–39
Greenberg, Daniel, 127
Greenspoon, Joel, 41, 46
Group approach to data, 70–71

Harford, R. A., 55, 113
Hecht, Selig, 126
Hefferline, Ralph F., 55, 113
Heisenberg, Werner, 46
Heredity, 87–88
Honesty in science, 100, 104
Hour, defined, 57–58, 86
Hull, Clark L., 61–62
Humility, need for in scientist, 36–37
Hunches, 69
Hunger, experimentally defined, 86
Hypothesis, 16; formulation and testing, 16, 32, 59, 68–69; myopia, 32–33
Hypothesitos, 69
Hypothetical constructs, 87–88
Hypothetical propositions, 59–60

Ideas, exchange of, 25
Individual approach to data, 69–71
Inductive process, 60–61
Informal discussions among scientists, 23–25
Informal theoretical method, 68–73
Information, exchange of, 25
Instrumentation, 40, 54–57, 90; reliability, 33–34
Interpretation of results, 34
Introspection, 41
Ivan, L. T., 104

James, William, 102
Jones, F. N., 83
Jones, M. H., 83
Journal of Experimental Medicine, 30–31
Journals, scientific, 20–23, 127–128; format of articles, 20, 21

Keenan, B., 55, 113
Kellner, Aaron, 26, 31–32
Kinsey report, 112
Kluckhohn, Clyde, 83

Kluckhohn, Florence, 102
Koch, Robert, 46
Kuhn, Thomas, 22, 66–67

Laboratory methods, 89–99; application to everyday world of, 89–99; criticism of, 90; informal discussions of, 25, 29
Lagrange, Joseph Louis, 36–37
Landreth, Catherine, 121
Lawfulness of events, 47, 68
Laws, scientific, 18
Learning, 87; programmed, 95
Light, measure of speed of, 33–34
Lodge, Sir Oliver, 50–52

Margenau, Henry, 40
Mars, description of, 18–19
Marx, Melvin H., 60, 78
Measurement, 38–39, 52–58; base in physical operation, 58; clocks, 57, 86; description and, 52; equal interval scale of, 52, 54; levels of, 86; nominal type of, 53–54, 74; ratio scale of, 54; thermometers, 55–57; types of, 74
Meetings, scientific, 25
Metaphysical theories, 62
Michelson, Albert A., 33–34
Models, human behavior, 97–98
Monkeys and chimpanzees, use of in research, 93
Moon, operational definition of, 84–85
Morley, Edward W., 33–34

Negative results, 28, 33–35
Newton, Isaac, 69

Observation, 16, 18, 38–47, 59–62, 84–85; correlation of specific, 84; definition of, 39; experiments and, 39–46; outside scientific boundaries and, 46; prediction from, 49–52; replication of, 41–43; requirements, 41

Operational approaches, 81–86, 129; criteria for, 82–83; formal symbols for, 80; objections to, 84–85; start with observation, 82
Oppenheimer, Robert, 132–133
Order, search for, 37, 39, 43, 46–49
Origin of Species, 23
Orne, Martin, 116

Packard, Vance, 122–123
Paradigms, in science, 66–67
Paranormal events, 43–45
Parapsychology, 42–45
Parsimony, problem of, 63; principle of, 63–64
Pasteur, Louis, 20, 38
Pattishall, Evan G., 114–115
Pauling, Linus, 15
Penicillin, discovery of, 16–17
Pigeons, use of in research, 91–93
Personality, 78–80
Pfeiffer, John, 127
Postulates, 61
Preconceived ideas, 32–35
Prediction, 38–39, 47–58; accuracy of, 50; definition of, 49; observation and experiment, 49–52; orbit of a fly, 50–51
Probability, concept of, 49, 101
Problem solving, 61
Pronko, N. H., 45
Proof, burden of, 46
Propositions, 59; empirical, 60; formal, 59; hypothetical, 60; theoretical, 60
Psychoanalytic theory, 62
Psychologists, public image, 122–123
Psychology, control of data, 71; experimental, 71–73; lack of data language, 41, 74; physics and, 40; scientific methodology, 40–46; theory construction, 68
Psychotherapy, definition of, 80
Published research, 20–21, 34

Quine, Willard S., 80–81

Rabbits, case of floppy-eared, 25–32

Rapoport, Anatol, 63, 81, 84–85

Rats, use of in research, 89–96

Records, research, 111, 112

Reichenbach, Hans, 78

Reinforcers, 23–24

Renan, Ernest, 47, 64, 127, 132

Representative design, 89, 111

Research, psychological, 15; as a career, 15; confidence of subject, 111–112; confidential material, 111–112; consent of subject, 112; deception in, 113–117; enjoyable aspects of, 20–21, 24–25; formal theoretical method of, 59–68; informal theoretical method of, 68–73; laws of, 19–20; methods of, 59–73; origin and development of, 15–17; planning, 20; precautions, 119; public concern with, 105–107; standard and acceptable procedures of, 109, 111–112, 119; stimuli to, 18–19

Results of research, 24, 34–35; interpretation of, 34; negative, 28, 34–35; presentation of, 34

Rostand, Jean, 127, 132

Russell, Bertrand, 79–80

Ryle, Gilbert, 46

Sampling procedures, 90

Scales, 53; nominal, 53–54; ordinal, 54; interval, equal, 54; ratio, 54

Science, orthodoxy of, 37; pure, 35

Scientific American, 23, 127

Scientific method, 15, 36, 59–60; characteristics, 36–38, 41; collection of data, 16; establishment of functional relationships, 16; observation, 16, 38–46; operational definitions, 16, 81–86; search for order, 17, 37, 39, 43, 46–49

Scientific papers, 20–21

Scientists, characteristics, 17, 36; citizen concern of, 104; communication among, 127–133; communication to public, 123–127, 132; contacts among, 25; curiosity of, 15; prepared mind of, 20; public image of, 122–123; religious beliefs of, 130; reputation of, 129; resistance to discovery of, 37, 129–131; social order of, 122–136

Serendipity, 25–32; definition of, 20

Sidman, Murray, 48, 65, 69, 70–73, 96, 129–130

Similarity, difference between analogy and, 99

Skinner, B. F., 17, 36–37, 68, 69, 74–75, 91–92, 95

Social order, science and, 133–136

Statistical techniques, 15, 90
Stevens, S. S., 85
Stone, L. J., 120
Stress, research on, 109–111
Subjective phenomena, 54
Swift, Jonathan, 19

Telepathy, 42
Telescopes, 9, 33
Temperature, measurement of, 55–57
Tests, psychological, 120–121
Textbooks, function of in science, 22–23
Theoretical method, 59; formal, 59–68; informal, 68–73
Theories, meaning of, 15; recognition of, 38; results conflicting with, 34–35
Theory construction, 59–73; criteria for testing, 63; data, 59–73; empirical propositions, 60; essentials, 61; formal method, 59; hypothetical propositions, 60; modifications of, 64; objections to, 65; theoretical propositions, 60; truth or falsity of, 62; verification of, 59, 63
Thermometers, 55–57
Thomas, Dylan, 162
Truth, scientific, 46–48, 62
Tuscany, Grand Duke of, 56

Uncertainty, principle of, 40–41
Understanding, as a scientific goal, 38
Underwood, B. J., 52
Uniformity of events, 47

Variables, 49, 73, 90; definition of, 74; intervening, 87–88
Verbal behavior, 23–24
Vision, study of, 93

Walter, W. Grey, 21
Wartofsky, M. W., 100
Weber, Max, 101
Wenger, Marion, 83

York, Archbishop of, 100, 132
Young, J. Z., 17